I0039893

Balancing the Scales

Understanding Criminal Sentencing

Lisa Stolzenberg and Stewart J. D'Alessio

Copyright © 2024 by Weston Publishing LLC

All rights reserved. No part of this book may be reproduced, stored in a retrieval system, or transmitted in any form or by any means— electronic, mechanical, photocopying, recording, or otherwise— without prior written permission from the publisher, except for brief quotations used in reviews or scholarly works.

ISBN: 978-1-936651-17-7 (paperback)
ISBN: 978-1-936651-18-4 (hardback)
ISBN: 978-1-936651-28-3 (ebook)

Printed in the United States of America

Use of AI

Publishing.ai was used as part of the manuscript development workflow for organizational and editorial support. The authors revised, reviewed and finalized the manuscript and assume full responsibility for its content.

Table of Contents

Introduction

In a dimly lit courtroom, a young man stands before a judge. His crime is serious but not uncommon: possession of a small amount of marijuana. The judge's gavel falls, and the sentence is announced: ten years in prison. The room gasps. The severity of the sentence appears disproportionate to the offense, highlighting the complexities and controversies inherent in criminal sentencing today. This case, like many others, raises questions about fairness, justice, and the purpose of our penal system.

This book aims to demystify the United States criminal sentencing process for both legal professionals and the general public. Sentencing is often shrouded in legal jargon and extensive, complicated guidelines, making it difficult for those outside the legal field to understand. Yet, it is a crucial element of our justice system, impacting millions of lives and communities. Through this book, we aim to bring clarity to this complex process.

Balancing the technical aspects of legal proceedings with accessible explanations for the benefit of a diverse audience, including college students and policymakers, is no easy task. However, it is a necessary one. By breaking down the principles of sentencing, examining real-life cases, and discussing potential reforms, this book seeks to provide a comprehensive yet approachable guide.

The book is organized into several chapters, each focusing on different facets of criminal sentencing. The first chapter delves into foundational principles, such as deterrence, retribution, and rehabilitation. The second chapter explores the sentencing process, detailing legal guidelines and the factors that influence judicial discretion. The third chapter presents case studies, offering insights into different sentencing outcomes and the reasoning behind them. The fourth chapter examines ethical and social considerations, including issues like biases and disparities. Finally, the fifth chapter addresses reform and future directions, and discusses current debates and alternatives to incarceration.

The need for sentencing reform is pressing. Studies show that the United States has one of the highest incarceration rates in the world. Mandatory minimums and three-strike laws have led to overcrowded prisons and a system that oftentimes prioritizes punishment over rehabilitation. By presenting key statistics and studies, this book sets the stage for discussions on how we can improve our sentencing system.

Our motivation for writing this book stems from a deep passion for helping all citizens understand the justice system. We believe that informed discussions on sentencing reform can lead to meaningful changes. As scholars who have spent years studying and teaching the legal system, we are committed to sharing insights that will hopefully both inspire and educate.

This book is primarily intended for college students and policymakers. It provides students with a foundation for their studies and encourages critical thinking about justice. It also offers policymakers insights that may influence their professional decisions and help promote equitable policies.

The research for this book was grounded in various sources, including legal texts, academic studies, and interviews with legal professionals. This variety ensures both credibility and depth, allowing readers to trust the information presented.

As you engage with this material, we encourage you to consider your role in advocating for a more equitable justice system. Whether you are a student, a policymaker, or simply someone interested in justice, your voice matters. Together, we can create a fair and just system that is reflective of our values. The journey to understanding and reform begins here.

Chapter 1:
The Foundations of Sentencing

In a world where justice is often seen through the lens of punishment, a judge's decision can ripple through society. Consider a case that recently made headlines. A corporate executive was convicted of embezzling millions, yet walked away with a sentence that many deemed a mere slap on the wrist: house arrest and community service. Meanwhile, others, for lesser crimes, are sentenced to years behind bars. Such disparities raise fundamental questions about the purpose and fairness of sentencing. Why do we punish, and what goals should our justice system strive to achieve? These are not just abstract inquiries but pressing concerns that shape lives and communities.

Understanding the foundations of sentencing requires a study of the philosophies that underpin it. Deterrence and retribution stand as the two primary pillars. Deterrence aims to prevent crime by instilling the fear of punishment. It's about sending a message to the individual offender as well as the society at large. Historically, deterrence has evolved from public spectacles of punishment to more subtle, systemic approaches. This theory suggests that by making an example of one, others will think twice before committing similar acts. Specific deterrence targets the individual, while general deterrence casts a wider net. However, these concepts, while seemingly straightforward, are fraught with challenges. The effectiveness of deterrence hinges on the certainty, severity, and swiftness of punishment. However, critics argue that it often fails to consider the complexities of human behavior and the socio-economic factors that drive crime.

Retribution, in contrast, is rooted in the idea of moral balance. Derived from the Latin word "tribution," meaning "I pay back," retributive justice posits that wrongdoers must suffer in proportion to their crimes. This notion has deep historical roots, reaching back to ancient laws such as the Law of Twelve Tables in Rome. Philosophers like Immanuel Kant championed the view that punishment should be meted out as a matter of moral duty, not necessarily to achieve practical ends like rehabilitation or deterrence. The core principles of retributive justice are simple yet profound: those who commit certain crimes deserve punishment, and it is morally right to deliver this punishment. Yet, this approach is not without its critics. Detractors point to the potential for disproportionate sentencing and the collateral damage inflicted on families and communities. They question whether retribution alone can truly serve the needs of justice.

When comparing deterrence and retribution, one discover a complex interplay of goals that sometimes conflict. Deterrence emphasizes future prevention, while retribution focuses on paying back for past actions. Balancing these aims requires careful consideration. For instance, a case involving a repeat offender might illustrate specific deterrence at play, as harsher penalties are imposed to prevent further infractions. Conversely, a one-time offender might face a sentence grounded more in retribution, reflecting the gravity of their actions rather than their likelihood of reoffending. In practice, sentencing often involves a mix of both philosophies, tailored to the specifics of each case.

To illustrate these concepts in action, consider two contrasting case studies. In one, a young man convicted of theft receives a lengthy prison sentence, ostensibly to deter others in his community. The decision sparks debate on whether the punishment fits the crime or merely serves as a warning. In the second scenario, a high-profile white-collar criminal is given a lighter sentence, justified by the argument that their crime, while serious, was non-violent and the individual poses little threat of recidivism. Here, retribution takes center stage, though critics argue it falls short of addressing the broader societal impact of the crime. These examples highlight the ongoing tension between deterrence and retribution, emphasizing the need for a justice system that balances both effectively.

As we explore the foundations of sentencing, it becomes clear that no single approach can address the multifaceted nature of crime and punishment. The challenge lies in crafting sentences that not only reflect the severity of the offense but also consider the potential for change and rehabilitation. This chapter seeks to unravel these complexities, offer insights into the theories that shape our legal landscape, and invite you to reflect on what justice truly means.

Rehabilitation and Restoration: Beyond Punishment

In the labyrinth that is the justice system, where punishment often takes center stage, the concepts of rehabilitation and restorative justice offer a path that looks beyond mere retribution. Rehabilitation aims to transform offenders into law-abiding citizens. It seeks to not only address the crime but also understand the underlying issues that led to it. Within the walls of correctional facilities, rehabilitation programs are designed to equip inmates with skills for reintegration into society. These programs range from educational courses and vocational training to therapy sessions that address behavioral and psychological issues. The goal is to reduce recidivism by providing offenders with the tools necessary for a productive future.

The effectiveness of rehabilitation is not just theoretical; real-world evidence supports its impact on reducing recidivism. Consider the case of a state correctional facility that implemented a comprehensive rehabilitation program. Inmates who participated were found to have significantly lower rates of reoffending than those who did not. Former inmates, once considered hardened criminals, have shared stories of transformation, attributing their new paths to the skills and support they received during incarceration. These success stories underscore the potential of rehabilitation to change lives and reduce crime, making a compelling case for its broader implementation in the justice system.

Restorative justice, in contrast, offers a different approach by focusing on healing rather than punishment. It brings together victims and offenders in a process that emphasizes accountability, reparation, and reconciliation. Through community-based programs and victim–offender mediation sessions, restorative justice seeks to address the harm caused by crime, foster understanding, and offer a chance for closure. In these settings, offenders gain insight into the impact of their actions, while victims express their feelings and needs. This dialogue can lead to agreements on how the offender might repair the harm, whether through community service, restitution, or other means. The benefits are evident in communities where such programs have been adopted and include reduced tension and a stronger sense of justice.

Integrating rehabilitation and restorative practices with traditional sentencing presents both challenges and opportunities. Hybrid sentencing models, which combine elements of punishment with restorative and rehabilitative measures, offer a promising approach. For instance, a judge might sentence an offender to a period of incarceration followed by mandatory participation in a restorative justice program. This approach allows for accountability while also addressing the root causes of criminal behavior. By incorporating these methods, the justice system can create more balanced sentences that not only punish but also promote healing and growth.

Reflective Exercise: Consider Your Community

Think about your community and identify any local programs that focus on rehabilitation or restorative justice. Reflect on how these programs might contribute to reducing crime and supporting both victims and offenders. If such programs are not present, consider why they might be beneficial and how they could be implemented.

In exploring the roles of rehabilitation and restorative justice, we see a shift from a purely punitive model to one that embraces healing and transformation. This shift reflects a growing understanding that true justice involves more than just punishment. It requires a commitment to addressing the harm caused by crime and offering hope for change. As we continue to examine these concepts, it's important to consider their implications for policy and practice, recognizing the potential they hold for creating a more equitable and effective justice system.

Dissecting the Sentencing Guidelines

Sentencing guidelines hold a central role in the criminal justice system, serving as a blueprint for judges to follow when determining sentences. Their primary purpose is to ensure that similar crimes receive similar punishments, thereby promoting fairness and consistency across different jurisdictions. These guidelines attempt to remove the guesswork from sentencing by providing a structured framework that considers the nature of the offense as well as the offender's criminal history. This standardization is crucial, as it helps to reduce the disparities that can arise from subjective sentencing. In practice, sentencing guidelines provide a balance between the need for uniformity and the necessity of individualization in justice.

Federal sentencing guidelines, in particular, have far-reaching influence. Established to create uniformity in sentencing at the federal level, these guidelines involve a complex matrix that calculates recommended sentences based on various factors. The system is designed to provide a range of permissible sentences, giving judges some leeway while maintaining a standard. However, the influence of these guidelines extends beyond merely suggesting a sentence. They shape the judicial process by setting expectations for what is deemed appropriate, thus impacting plea bargains and other pre-trial negotiations. These guidelines, though advisory, carry significant weight, and judges often adhere closely to them to avoid appeals and ensure perceived fairness.

The practical application of sentencing guidelines in courtrooms reveals their strengths and shortcomings. In theory, they aim to eliminate bias by anchoring sentences in established criteria. However, real-world application often diverges from this ideal. Case studies illustrate instances where guidelines have either constrained judicial discretion or failed to account for unique circumstances. For example, in a case involving drug trafficking, the guidelines might suggest a harsh sentence based solely on the quantity of drugs, ignoring mitigating factors such as the defendant's personal history or potential for rehabilitation. Such rigidity can lead to sentences that feel unjust or out of proportion with the crime.

Critics of sentencing guidelines often point to their inflexibility and the resultant lack of fairness. Strict adherence to guidelines can strip judges of the ability to tailor sentences to individual cases, leading to outcomes that may not align with the principles of justice. This rigidity is especially problematic in cases with complex circumstances that the guidelines fail to anticipate. Critics argue that while guidelines strive for consistency, they sometimes do so at the expense of fairness and humanity. The concern is that a one-size-fits-all approach cannot adequately address the nuances of every case.

Recent reforms in sentencing guidelines aim to address these criticisms by incorporating more flexibility and discretion. Legislative amendments have been introduced to allow judges greater latitude in deviating from guidelines when circumstances warrant it. These changes reflect a growing recognition of the need for a more nuanced approach to sentencing, one that balances the benefits of standardization with the necessity for individualized justice. By introducing reforms, lawmakers hope to strike a better balance between consistency and fairness, ensuring that the justice system can adapt to the complexities of modern crime and punishment.

Case Study: A Judge's Quandary

Consider a case where a judge faces a defendant charged with a non-violent drug offense. The guidelines recommend a lengthy prison term, yet the defendant is a first-time offender with strong community ties and a history of addiction. The judge, recognizing the potential for rehabilitation, opts to impose a sentence that includes drug treatment and community service instead of incarceration. This decision, while deviating from the guidelines, highlights the importance of judicial discretion in achieving just outcomes and underscores the ongoing debate on the role of guidelines in the justice system.

How Sentencing Influences Recidivism Rates

The link between sentencing and recidivism is a complex tapestry that reflects the broader challenges of the criminal justice system. Recidivism, simply put, is the tendency of a convicted criminal to reoffend. It is a critical measure of the effectiveness of sentencing practices. Studies have shown that the length and type of sentences can significantly influence recidivism rates. Longer sentences, contrary to what one might assume, do not always deter future crimes. In fact, research suggests that excessively long incarcerations may increase the likelihood of reoffending. This is because extended imprisonment can disrupt social ties, reduce employment prospects, and expose inmates to environments that foster criminal behavior. The social and psychological impact of long-term imprisonment often leaves individuals ill-prepared to reintegrate into society, thus perpetuating the cycle of crime.

Conversely, alternative sentencing methods, such as community service, have shown promise in reducing recidivism. Community service offers a way for offenders to give back to society, fostering a sense of responsibility and connection to the community. This approach not only mitigates the isolating effects of incarceration but also provides offenders with valuable life skills and work experience. The hands-on nature of community service can serve as a practical deterrent, encouraging offenders to avoid future criminal activity by highlighting the consequences of their actions. By remaining engaged with their community, individuals can maintain support networks that are crucial for successful reintegration.

Innovative approaches like drug courts have also emerged as effective tools in reducing recidivism, particularly for non-violent drug offenders. Drug courts focus on rehabilitation rather than punishment, offering offenders the opportunity to receive treatment and support for substance abuse issues. This approach recognizes addiction as a root cause of criminal behavior and seeks to address it directly. By providing a structured environment that combines judicial oversight with treatment programs, drug courts have significantly reduced recidivism rates among participants. The success of these courts underscores the importance of addressing the underlying issues that lead to crime, rather than solely focusing on punitive measures.

Another promising alternative to traditional incarceration is electronic monitoring. This method allows individuals to serve their sentences while remaining in their communities, albeit under strict supervision. Electronic monitoring can include GPS tracking and regular check-ins with authorities to ensure compliance with the terms of the sentence. By allowing offenders to maintain employment and family connections, electronic monitoring helps reduce the factors that contribute to recidivism, such as unemployment and social isolation. The use of technology in this way balances the need for accountability with the benefits of community-based rehabilitation.

Socio-economic factors play a significant role in determining recidivism rates. Access to post-release support services, such as housing assistance and job training, is crucial for reducing the likelihood of reoffending. However, many former inmates struggle to find stable employment upon release due to gaps in their work history and the stigma associated with having a criminal record. Employment opportunities, although vital for the successful reintegration of ex-offenders, are therefore often scarce. Without stable employment and housing, individuals are more likely to return to criminal activity as a means of survival. This cycle highlights the need for comprehensive support systems that address the economic and social barriers faced by those reentering society.

In light of these factors, it is clear that to make sentencing decisions, judges must consider more than just the severity of the crime. They must address the broader context in which offenders live and operate. By adopting a more holistic approach to sentencing, one that includes alternative methods and support services, we can reduce recidivism and promote long-term public safety. The challenge lies in balancing the need for accountability with the potential for rehabilitation, ensuring that every sentence serves not just as a punishment but also as a pathway to a better future.

The Role of Judicial Discretion in Sentencing

Judicial discretion is a cornerstone of the sentencing process, where judges hold the power to determine the nature and extent of punishment within the boundary of the law. It allows for flexibility, enabling judges to tailor sentences based on the unique circumstances of each case, rather than adhering strictly to predetermined rules. This personal judgment recognizes that no two cases are identical, even when the charges are similar. Historically, judicial discretion has been rooted in the common law tradition, where judges have long exercised judgment to balance the scales of justice. The latitude granted to judges aims to ensure that sentences are fair and just, that factors such as the offender's background, the context of the crime, and the offender's potential for rehabilitation, are taken into account. However, this power is not without its complexities.

The benefits of judicial discretion are evident in its ability to foster fairness and account for individual differences. By allowing judges to consider various factors, discretion can lead to more equitable outcomes that reflect the nuances of each situation. For example, a judge might choose a lighter sentence for a first-time offender, recognizing the offender's potential for rehabilitation and the mitigating circumstances surrounding the crime. Yet, this same discretion can result in disparities, where similar offenses receive vastly different sentences based on the presiding judge's perspective. Such variability raises concerns about consistency and fairness, leading to perceptions of judicial bias. Instances of perceived bias can occur when judges' personal beliefs or unconscious biases influence their decisions, resulting in sentences that may not align with societal norms of justice.

To guide judicial discretion and mitigate these challenges, various frameworks and guidelines have been developed. Sentencing councils, for example, have provided recommendations and established standards to promote uniformity in sentencing practices. These councils aim to balance the need for consistency with the flexibility required to consider individual case factors. By offering a structured framework, they help reduce the potential for bias while preserving judges' ability to tailor sentences. Additionally, training programs and continuing education opportunities for judges focus on raising awareness regarding implicit biases and promoting equitable decision-making. These mechanisms seek to ensure that discretion is exercised fairly and justly, fostering trust in the judicial process.

Real-world examples illustrate the profound impact of judicial discretion on sentencing outcomes. Consider the case of a non-violent drug offender who faced a lengthy prison term under strict sentencing guidelines. The judge, exercising discretion and recognizing the offender's potential for change and the circumstances that led to the offense, chose instead to impose a sentence involving rehabilitation and community service. This decision highlights the positive use of discretion to achieve a more rehabilitative outcome. In contrast, high-profile cases have also showcased the pitfalls of discretion. In one instance, a judge's lenient sentencing of a wealthy defendant for a serious crime sparked public outrage, as many perceived the decision to be influenced by the defendant's social status. These cases underscore the dual nature of discretion, emphasizing the need for careful consideration and responsible use.

The role of judicial discretion in sentencing is a delicate balance between fairness and consistency. It empowers judges to craft sentences that reflect the complexities of human behavior and the justice system's goals. However, it also necessitates vigilant oversight and ongoing efforts to minimize bias and ensure equity. As we continue to explore the intricacies of sentencing, the significance of discretion remains clear, shaping outcomes in ways that can both inspire and challenge our understanding of justice.

Understanding Mandatory Minimums and Their Impact

Mandatory minimum sentencing laws have become a cornerstone of the American legal system, emerging from a desire to impose strict penalties on certain offenses. These laws originated in the 1980s, a time marked by a heightened focus on law and order. Legislators, aiming to combat rising crime rates and drug epidemics, crafted these laws to remove judicial discretion and ensure uniformity and severity in sentencing. The intent was clear: create a deterrent effect by guaranteeing that certain crimes, such as drug offenses and violent crimes involving firearms, would result in predetermined, non-negotiable prison terms. By doing so, lawmakers believed they could curb crime and send a strong message to potential offenders.

Despite their intended purpose, mandatory minimums have sparked significant debate over their impact on fairness within the justice system. Critics argue that these laws often lead to disproportionate sentencing outcomes, where the punishment does not adequately fit the crime. This is especially evident in cases involving low-level drug offenders who receive the same harsh sentences as major traffickers. Such rigidity disregards the nuances of individual cases, stripping judges of the ability to consider factors like the offenders' role in the crime, their background, or their potential for rehabilitation. As a result, mandatory minimums have been criticized for contributing to a justice system that appears more focused on punishment rather than on equitable justice.

The implications of mandatory minimums extend beyond individual cases, contributing significantly to prison overcrowding across the United States. With sentences that mandate long periods of incarceration, the prison population has swelled, placing immense pressure on correctional facilities. This overcrowding exacerbates conditions within prisons, stretching resources thin and often limiting access to rehabilitation and education programs that could aid in reducing recidivism. Furthermore, the demographic impact is stark, with minority communities disproportionately affected by these laws. Studies have shown that Black individuals are more likely to receive mandatory minimum sentences than their white counterparts, exacerbating racial disparities in incarceration rates and further fueling calls for reform.

In recent years, the conversation around mandatory minimums has shifted, with growing recognition of their flaws and the need for reform. Advocacy groups and legal experts have been vocal in their calls for change, arguing that these laws do more harm than good. Organizations like The Sentencing Project have highlighted the negative impacts of mandatory minimums and have pushed for legislative changes that would restore judicial discretion. These efforts have yielded some results, with certain states revising or eliminating mandatory minimums for specific offenses, particularly drug-related crimes. Legislative proposals at both the state and federal levels aim to soften the rigidity of these laws, promoting alternatives that focus on prevention, early intervention, and rehabilitation rather than extended incarceration.

As discussions around mandatory minimums continue, it is crucial to consider the broader implications of these laws on the justice system. The challenge lies in finding a balance between maintaining public safety and ensuring that sentences are fair and just. By exploring alternatives and engaging in informed debate, there is potential to create a system that is not only effective but also equitable. The push for reform reflects a growing awareness that the justice system must evolve to meet the needs of society, emphasizing rehabilitation and fairness alongside accountability.

Reflecting on mandatory minimums and their impact, we are reminded of the importance of having a justice system that serves all its citizens equitably. As we consider the future of sentencing, the lessons learned from the past and the voices calling for change will guide us toward a more just and balanced approach to criminal justice.

Chapter 2:
The Sentencing Process

Imagine this scene: Inside a bustling courtroom, there's an air of anticipation. The defendant sits silently at the defense table, eyes fixed on the judge, who is poised to make a decision that could alter the course of several lives. This is the sentencing hearing, a pivotal moment in the criminal justice process where the complexities of law, human emotion, and societal norms converge. Understanding this process is crucial for anyone seeking to comprehend how justice is administered, be it a college student studying criminal justice or a policymaker looking to shape future laws.

A sentencing hearing begins with opening statements from both the prosecution and defense. These initial remarks set the stage for what will follow, providing a roadmap of the arguments each side intends to present. The prosecutor typically goes first, outlining the severity of the crime and the punishment they believe is warranted. Following this, the defense attorney takes the floor, often emphasizing mitigating factors that may warrant a more lenient sentence. This back-and-forth establishes the framework for the evidence and testimonies that will later be presented. It is a strategic dance, with each side aiming to sway the judge's perspective in their favor.

Throughout the hearing, the roles of key participants come into sharp focus. The judge, tasked with overseeing the proceedings, listens intently to the arguments presented. They are the ultimate arbiter, responsible for ensuring that justice is served while adhering to legal standards and guidelines. Meanwhile, the defense attorney acts as the advocate for the defendant, striving to highlight any factors that might lead to a more lenient sentence. They may call upon witnesses, introduce evidence, and argue for alternative sentencing options. Each participant plays a critical role in shaping the outcome, with their contributions forming the backbone of the hearing.

One of the most poignant moments in a sentencing hearing is the delivery of victim impact statements. These statements offer victims a voice, allowing them to articulate the profound effects the crime has had on their lives. According to Section 722(1) of the Criminal Code of Canada, courts must consider the physical, emotional, and economic harm suffered by victims. These narratives can be deeply moving, providing the judge with a personal glimpse into the crime's impact beyond the legal facts. Emotional appeals and factual details intertwine, offering a powerful counterpoint to the legal arguments. The judge weighs these statements carefully, as they provide critical insights that might not be evident through legal arguments alone.

As the hearing progresses to its final deliberation and sentencing phase, the judge's role becomes even more significant. They must sift through the evidence, arguments, and emotional testimonies to reach a decision that aligns with both the law and broader principles of justice. This process, known as judicial deliberation, involves consideration of the statutory limits, the defendant's criminal history, and the presence of any mitigating or aggravating circumstances. The judge must balance the need for punishment with the potential for rehabilitation, often deliberating on what sentence will serve the interests of justice most effectively.

Reflection Section: Considering Perspectives

As you think about the complexities of a sentencing hearing, consider the perspectives of each participant. How might their roles and responsibilities influence the outcome? Reflect on how these different viewpoints contribute to the overall process of justice.

Ultimately, the sentencing hearing is a microcosm of the justice system itself, where law, emotion, and human experience intersect. It is a process that demands both precision and empathy, challenging those involved to seek a balance between the letter of the law and the spirit of justice.

The Mitigating and Aggravating Factors in Sentencing

Mitigating and aggravating factors play crucial roles in determining the final outcome when it comes to sentencing. These factors can either lessen or intensify the severity of a sentence based on the specifics of a case. Mitigating factors refer to those that might lead to a reduced sentence. They typically include circumstances such as a defendant's lack of prior criminal history, their role in the offense, or personal conditions like mental health issues. For instance, if a defendant committed a crime under duress or coercion, the court might consider this a mitigating factor. In contrast, aggravating factors increase the severity of a sentence. These include the use of violence, the involvement of weapons, or if the crime was particularly heinous. A repeat-offender status also serves as a powerful aggravating factor, often leading to harsher penalties.

Exploring specific cases highlights how mitigating factors can alter sentencing outcomes. Consider a scenario where a defendant suffers from a mental health disorder, which played a significant role in their criminal behavior. A judge, upon reviewing psychological evaluations and expert testimonies, might consider the defendant's actions a result of their mental state rather than an intentional criminal conduct. In such cases, the sentence might lean toward rehabilitation rather than punishment. The court may order treatment instead of jail time, aiming to address the root cause of the behavior. This approach not only offers the possibility of rehabilitation but also acknowledges the complexities of human behavior that pure punishment often overlooks.

Conversely, aggravating factors, when present, tend to tip the scales toward more severe sentencing. A case involving armed robbery is an apt example. Here, the use of a weapon significantly worsens the crime in the eyes of the law. The potential for harm increases, and the court often responds with a stiffer penalty. Similarly, habitual offenders who consistently engage in criminal activities face harsher sentences due to the perceived threat they pose to society. A history of crime suggests a pattern that courts aim to disrupt through more rigorous punitive measures, reflecting the need to protect the community and deter future offenses.

Effectively presenting these factors during sentencing hearings is a strategic endeavor for both defense and prosecution. Defense attorneys must craft persuasive arguments that highlight mitigating factors, using evidence and testimonies to paint a comprehensive picture of the defendant's circumstances. This involves gathering character references and demonstrating the defendant's potential for reform; for example, showcasing a strong support network or a commitment to making amends can persuade a judge to consider alternatives to incarceration. On the prosecutorial side, emphasizing aggravating factors requires recounting in detail the crime's impact and severity. Prosecutors might focus on the premeditated nature of an offense or the defendant's disregard for the law, urging the court to impose a sentence that reflects the gravity of the crime.

Case Study Reflection: Weighing Factors

Consider a hypothetical case where a young adult is charged with burglary but has a history of substance abuse and no prior convictions. How might a defense attorney use these mitigating factors to influence the judge's decision? Conversely, if the crime involved the use of force or resulted in significant harm to the victim, how would the prosecutor argue for a more severe sentence? Reflect on how these factors interplay to shape the final judgment.

The nuanced interplay of mitigating and aggravating factors underscores the complexity of sentencing. Each case presents a unique set of circumstances, challenging the court to balance empathy with justice. The ability of legal representatives to effectively argue these factors can significantly sway the final decision, emphasizing the need for a thorough understanding of both the law and the human stories behind each case.

The Sentencing Memorandum: Crafting Persuasive Arguments

In the nuanced dance of legal proceedings, the sentencing memorandum stands as a pivotal document, weaving the threads of a case into a cohesive narrative that influences the judge's final decision. At its core, a sentencing memorandum serves to outline the defense's arguments for a particular sentence, summarizing critical points that either advocate for leniency or propose alternative sentencing options. This document typically includes a narrative section, which details the defendant's personal history, circumstances surrounding the offense, and any mitigating factors that may warrant a more lenient sentence. Additionally, it often incorporates legal arguments that reference statutes, case law, and sentencing guidelines, thereby grounding the defense's position in established legal precedent. Together, these components create a compelling case for the judge's consideration during sentencing deliberations, providing a structured argument that highlights the nuances of the defendant's situation.

To craft a persuasive sentencing memorandum, attorneys must employ a blend of strategic narrative and robust evidence. One effective strategy involves the use of character references and expert testimonies. Character references from family, friends, or community members can paint a picture of the defendant's character beyond the crime, emphasizing positive attributes and their potential for rehabilitation. These personal accounts humanize the defendant, offering the judge a more comprehensive view of the individual behind the charges. Meanwhile, expert testimonies provide professional insights that may elucidate factors such as mental health issues and the socio-economic pressures that contributed to the offense. By integrating these elements, attorneys can build a multi-faceted argument that resonates on both emotional and rational levels.

Supporting evidence serves as the backbone of any sentencing memorandum, lending credibility and substance to the arguments presented. Thorough documentation, including medical and psychological reports, plays an instrumental role in reinforcing claims made by the defense. For instance, if a defendant struggles with mental health issues, psychological evaluations can substantiate this, demonstrating how these challenges may have influenced their behavior. Similarly, medical reports can highlight any physical conditions that might impact the defendant's ability to endure a particular sentence. Meticulously collecting and presenting such evidence ensures that the judge has a clear understanding of the defendant's circumstances, which can significantly sway the sentencing outcome.

Examining case studies of impactful sentencing memoranda reveals the profound influence such documents can have on judicial decisions. For example, a young woman was convicted of drug offenses. Her attorney submitted a sentencing memorandum that included a detailed account of her struggles with addiction, supported by testimonials from her rehabilitation counselors and a comprehensive psychological assessment. This document highlighted her progress in treatment and her commitment to recovery, ultimately persuading the judge to opt for a sentence that prioritized rehabilitation over incarceration. In another instance, a defendant charged with a non-violent financial crime had a memorandum bolstered by character references from his employer and colleagues, alongside evidence of his efforts to make restitution. These compelling arguments led to a sentence involving community service and restitution payments, rather than prison time.

Ultimately, the art of crafting a sentencing memorandum lies in its ability to weave a narrative that captures the essence of the defendant's story while grounding it in legal rationale and factual evidence. It is a delicate balance between persuasion and precision, where every word plays a role in shaping the judge's perception. The document must resonate beyond the walls of the courtroom, echoing the complexities of human behavior and the offender's potential for redemption. By carefully constructing these memoranda, attorneys not only advocate for their clients but also contribute to a broader dialogue about justice, fairness, and the capacity for change within the legal system.

Probation Officers: The Unsung Heroes of Sentencing

In the often overlooked layers of the criminal justice system, probation officers emerge as critical figures, quietly influencing the sentencing process behind the scenes. Their role is multifaceted, encompassing responsibilities that extend well beyond the supervision of offenders. One of their primary duties is conducting pre-sentence investigations, a task that involves gathering comprehensive information about the defendant. These investigations are not merely perfunctory, as they delve into the defendant's criminal history and personal background, as well as the circumstances surrounding the offense. Through interviews, research, and collaboration with other agencies, probation officers compile detailed profiles which become the foundation upon which pre-sentence reports are built, providing judges with essential insights that inform sentencing decisions.

Preparing pre-sentence reports is a meticulous process, akin to piecing together a complex puzzle. These reports encompass several components, each contributing to a holistic view of the defendant. They include a summary of the crime, the defendant's personal and family history, and any prior criminal conduct. Psychological evaluations, employment records, and educational background are often woven into the narrative, painting a comprehensive picture of the individual. Probation officers must ensure that their reports are thorough and objective, presenting an unbiased account that aids the court in determining an appropriate sentence. The importance of these reports cannot be overstated, as they serve as a crucial tool in the court's decision-making arsenal.

Collaboration between probation officers and judges is integral to the sentencing process. Probation officers act as intermediaries, providing judges with the contextual understanding necessary to make informed decisions. This relationship is built on trust and professionalism, as probation officers often conduct interviews with defendants and their families to gather first-hand information. These interactions offer a glimpse into the defendant's life that may not be apparent through legal documents alone. The insights gained from these interviews help judges grasp the nuances of each case, enabling them to tailor sentences that reflect both the severity of the crime and the potential for rehabilitation. This way, probation officers contribute to a more nuanced and empathetic approach to justice, bridging the gap between the defendant's personal circumstances and the courtroom.

The impact of probation officer recommendations on sentencing outcomes is profound, often swaying the final decision in significant ways. A well-drafted report with cogent recommendations can lead to completely different sentencing options, such as probation or community service, instead of incarceration. Consider a case where a probation officer's report highlighted the defendant's commitment to rehabilitation efforts, including their consistent attendance at therapy sessions and positive community involvement. This information, presented compellingly, persuaded the judge to opt for a sentence that emphasized continued rehabilitation instead of prison time. Alternatively, reports that underscore risk factors, such as a history of reoffending or a lack of remorse, might lead to stricter sentences. The weight of these recommendations underscores the pivotal role probation officers play in shaping sentencing outcomes, often serving as the linchpin that balances punishment with rehabilitation.

Despite their behind-the-scenes role, probation officers are indispensable to the justice system, providing the insights and recommendations that guide judicial decisions. Their work ensures that sentencing is not just a mechanical application of the law but a thoughtful consideration of the individual at the heart of the case. By recognizing their contributions, we appreciate the nuanced tapestry of justice, where each thread—be it legal, personal, or rehabilitative—plays a critical role in the broader narrative of criminal sentencing.

The Psychological and Emotional Journey of Judges

Sentencing, a critical juncture in the judicial process, demands more than legal acumen from judges; it calls for a delicate balance between their personal beliefs and professional obligations. When tasked with determining a sentence, judges must sift through a myriad of factors, from the gravity of the crime to the offender's potential for rehabilitation. This process is not only an intellectual one but also a significant emotional and psychological undertaking. Judges often find themselves wrestling with their own moral compass while adhering to the rigid structures of the law. They must set aside personal biases and focus instead on fairness and the principles of justice that guide their profession. This mental balancing act is further complicated by the weight of knowing that their decisions will have lasting impacts on the lives of the defendants, victims, and broader community.

High-profile cases amplify these challenges, often placing judges under the intense scrutiny of public opinion and media narratives. In such cases, the courtroom becomes a stage where every decision is dissected by both the media and society at large. Judges may face pressure to conform to public expectations, whether in the form of harsher penalties due to societal outrage or leniency in the face of public sympathy. Moreover, the media's portrayal of a case can sway public sentiment, adding an external layer of pressure that judges must navigate while maintaining impartiality. This scrutiny can lead to a heightened sense of responsibility, as judges strive to render decisions that not only uphold justice but also withstand public examination. The challenge lies in remaining steadfast in their duty to interpret the law objectively, without succumbing to the noise of public discourse.

To manage the stress and maintain impartiality amid such pressures, judges often rely on a range of coping mechanisms and support systems. Peer support groups offer a crucial outlet, providing a space for judges to discuss their experiences and share insights with colleagues who understand the unique pressures of the bench. These groups foster a sense of camaraderie and mutual support, helping judges in processing the emotional toll of their responsibilities. Additionally, some judges turn to mindfulness practices or professional counseling to manage stress and maintain mental clarity. Such strategies are vital in ensuring that judges continue to perform their duties with the objectivity and fairness that justice demands. The psychological resilience developed through these practices is as essential as legal expertise in the execution of their duties.

Real-life case studies reveal the emotional complexity that judges face when making difficult sentencing decisions. For instance, in cases involving young offenders, judges often grapple with balancing accountability and the potential for rehabilitation. One judge reflected on a case where a teenager was involved in a serious crime, noting the internal conflict between the desire to offer a chance for reform and the need to uphold justice for the victims. This reflection highlights the profound impact that such decisions have on judges, who must weigh their legal obligations against the human stories that underpin each case. Another judge recounted the challenges of sentencing in cases with significant media attention, where public sentiment clash with the legal realities of the case. These reflections underscore the intricate dance between emotion and logic that defines the judicial role in sentencing.

Through this lens, we see that the role of a judge extends far beyond the mere interpretation of law to encompass a deep engagement with the human elements of justice, requiring a level of empathy and introspection that is both demanding and rewarding. Judges, in their pursuit of justice, must continually reconcile the law with the lived realities of those who stand before them, navigating a path that is fraught with challenges yet driven by an unwavering commitment to fairness and integrity.

Navigating Plea Bargains and Sentencing Outcomes

Plea bargaining is a pivotal mechanism within the criminal justice system, serving as a tool that prosecutors and defense attorneys wield to resolve cases efficiently. At its core, a plea bargain is an agreement wherein a defendant pleads guilty to a lesser charge or receives a lighter sentence in exchange for concessions from the prosecution. This process often involves the defendant agreeing to provide information or testify against co-defendants. There are several types of plea bargains: charge bargaining, where the defendant pleads guilty to a lesser charge; sentence bargaining, which involves negotiating a lighter sentence; and fact bargaining, where certain facts are agreed upon to avoid more severe charges. Each type reflects strategic negotiations between defense and prosecution with the aim of reaching a consensus that benefits both parties while ensuring the case does not proceed to a lengthy trial.

Plea bargains have notable advantages and disadvantages within the justice system. On the one hand, they expedite case resolution, significantly reducing court backlogs and ensuring that justice is delivered swiftly. This efficiency allows courts to allocate resources to more complex cases that necessitate full trials. On the other hand, the practice of plea bargaining can sometimes lead to coercion, where defendants feel pressured to accept a bargain to avoid the risk of harsher penalties at trial. This pressure is particularly intense for those who lack resources for a robust defense. The potential for injustice looms large, as innocent defendants might plead guilty to crimes they did not commit to escape the uncertainty and severity of a potential trial outcome.

The negotiation process in plea bargaining is a delicate dance between the defense and prosecution. Initially, the prosecution presents an offer, laying out the terms of the bargain. This proposal stems from a strategic assessment of the case's strengths and weaknesses, including the evidence and witness credibility. The defense then evaluates the offer, weighing the risks of going to trial against the benefits of accepting the plea. Defense attorneys aim to negotiate terms that minimize their client's exposure to severe penalties. This often involves emphasizing mitigating factors or highlighting weaknesses in the prosecution's case. Once both parties reach an agreement, the plea bargain is presented to the judge for approval, marking a pivotal moment wherein the agreed-upon terms become binding.

Plea bargains have a profound impact on sentencing trends, shaping how justice is administered across the system. Statistically, the majority of criminal cases are resolved through plea bargains rather than trials. This prevalence affects broader sentencing patterns, as negotiated outcomes often result in sentences lighter than those handed down after a trial. Reliance on plea bargains can create a system where outcomes are less about the pursuit of justice and more about negotiated compromise. This shift raises questions about the role of plea bargains in a fair legal system, as they can both streamline efficiency and obscure the true nature of justice.

As we conclude Chapter 2, the intricate web of the sentencing process becomes clearer. From the emotional weight of victim impact statements to the strategic negotiations of plea bargains, each element plays a crucial role in shaping justice. Understanding these facets is essential for anyone engaged with the legal system, whether as a student, policymaker, or legal professional. The next chapter will delve into real-world case studies, offering a deeper look at how these processes unfold in practice and their implications for justice and the society.

Chapter 3:
Case Studies – Real-World Sentencing Scenarios

Consider the courtroom as a stage, where the drama of justice unfolds in full view of the public eye. High-profile cases captivate the media and audiences alike, shaping perceptions of fairness and justice. One such case is that of Bernie Madoff, whose Ponzi scheme defrauded thousands of investors out of billions of dollars. When Madoff stood before the judge, the world watched with bated breath. The sentence—150 years in prison—was as much about punishing Madoff as it was about sending a message. This decision reflected the gravity of his crimes and the outrage his actions had provoked. It was an unprecedented sentence, intended to serve as a deterrent to others in the financial sector. Madoff's sentencing was not just about one man's guilt; it was an exposition of the justice system's response to white-collar crime on a massive scale.

In stark contrast, the case of Brock Turner brought a different kind of public scrutiny. Turner, a Stanford University swimmer, was convicted of sexually assaulting an unconscious woman. The judge sentenced him to six months in county jail, a decision that sparked widespread public outrage. Many felt the sentence was too lenient, given the severity of the crime and its impact on the victim. The judge cited Turner's age and lack of criminal history as reasons for the light sentence, arguing that a longer prison term would have a severe impact on his life. This reasoning, however, was met with backlash, as it seemed to prioritize the future of the perpetrator over the trauma endured by the victim. The case highlighted perceived disparities in the justice system, where factors such as privilege and social standing appeared to influence outcomes.

Judicial reasoning in such high-profile cases often involves a complex interplay of legal precedents and societal expectations. In Madoff's case, the judge drew upon the need for a strong deterrent effect in financial crimes, applying precedent to justify an extraordinarily harsh sentence. The primary goal here was to uphold the integrity of the financial system and restore public confidence. In Turner's case, the application of precedent was less clear-cut, with the judge emphasizing rehabilitation over retribution. This decision sparked debate about the balance between judicial discretion and mandatory sentencing guidelines and whether the latter could have led to a different outcome.

The societal and legal implications of these cases are profound. Madoff's sentence led to increased scrutiny of financial regulations and calls for stricter oversight of investment activities. It underscored the necessity of holding powerful individuals accountable, regardless of their status. Conversely, the Turner case spurred legislative changes aimed at addressing sexual assault sentencing. California lawmakers responded by passing a bill mandating minimum sentences for certain sexual offenses, reflecting the public's demand for more stringent penalties. These legislative changes illustrate how public reaction can drive policy reform, highlighting the dynamic relationship between high-profile cases and the evolution of the law.

Media coverage plays a vital role in shaping the narrative and public perception of these cases. The extensive media attention that surrounded Madoff's case framed it as a cautionary tale of greed and corruption, influencing public opinion and affirming the justice system's capacity to deliver severe punishment for financial crimes. In Turner's case, media portrayal emphasized the perceived inequities in sentencing, with headlines focusing on the leniency shown to a privileged college athlete. This coverage fueled public discourse on systemic bias and the need for sentencing reform, demonstrating the media's power to amplify public sentiment and prompt legislative action.

Media Influence Reflection Exercise

Reflect on how media coverage influenced your perception of these cases. Consider the role of headlines, news stories, and social media in shaping your understanding of justice. How might your views differ if the media had portrayed these cases in a different light? Think about the potential impact of media bias and how it affects your perception of fairness in high-profile sentencing decisions.

Sentencing in Cases of Violent Crimes: A Balancing Act

Sentencing violent offenders presents unique challenges for the criminal justice system, as these cases often involve serious harm to individuals or communities, making public safety a significant concern. Judges must weigh the need for punishment against the potential for rehabilitation, a balance that is not always easy to achieve. Violent crimes, by their nature, evoke strong emotional responses, from both the victims and the public. The impact on victims can be profound, affecting their physical and emotional well-being long after the crime has been committed. This makes victim impact statements a powerful element in the sentencing process, as they provide the court with a vivid account of the crime's consequences. These statements can sway judicial decisions, tipping the scales toward harsher sentences in an effort to honor the victim's experience.

Consider the sentencing of serial offenders, who pose a persistent threat to public safety due to their repeated criminal behavior. These cases often result in lengthy prison terms, as judges strive to protect society from further harm. However, such sentences also raise questions about the potential for rehabilitation. Is it possible to reform an individual who has consistently demonstrated a pattern of violence? This question is central to the sentencing process, as judges must decide whether the offender can realistically be reintegrated into society. High-profile murder cases further complicate this equation, as they often draw intense media scrutiny and public pressure for severe penalties. In these situations, judges must navigate the fine line between delivering justice and responding to public demands, all while considering the individual circumstances of the offender.

Victim impact statements play a crucial role in informing these decisions, offering a personal perspective that goes beyond the mere facts of the case. They allow victims to express how the crime has altered their lives, providing a human element that can deeply influence the sentencing outcome. Judges must carefully balance these narratives with the legal principles of justice and fairness, ensuring that the sentence reflects both the crime's severity and the offender's potential for rehabilitation. The integration of rehabilitation programs into sentencing decisions represents an effort to address these complexities. Such programs aim to provide offenders with the tools and support needed to change their behavior, reducing their likelihood of committing future crimes. By focusing on rehabilitation, the justice system acknowledges the potential for growth and transformation, even in cases involving violent crimes.

Balancing punishment and rehabilitation also extends to the broader societal implications of sentencing decisions. A harsh sentence may satisfy the public's desire for retribution, but it may not necessarily contribute to long-term safety if it neglects the root causes of criminal behavior. Conversely, a rehabilitative approach may offer the offender a chance to reform but can be perceived as being insufficiently punitive by those affected by the crime. Consequently, judges are tasked with finding a middle ground and crafting sentences that address both the immediate needs of justice and the long-term goal of reducing recidivism. This delicate balance requires a deep understanding of human behavior, the law, and the societal context in which these crimes occur. Each case presents its own set of challenges, demanding careful consideration and an unwavering commitment to fairness and justice.

White-Collar Crimes: Sentencing Disparities and Their Causes

White-collar crimes often conjure images of sophisticated operations led by individuals in high offices, manipulating systems for personal gain. Yet, when it comes to sentencing, these crimes frequently receive what many perceive as lenient treatment compared to their violent counterparts. This perception stems from several factors, including the non-violent nature of these offenses and the societal status of the offenders. Unlike violent crimes, which evoke immediate emotional responses and concerns for public safety, white-collar crimes often unfold over time, with their effects—though equally devastating—impacting victims in less visible ways. The disparity in sentencing between white-collar and violent crimes raises critical questions about justice and equity. While a violent offender might face years behind bars, a white-collar criminal might receive probation or a short prison sentence, despite the significant financial harm inflicted.

Examining prominent cases further illustrates these disparities. The Enron scandal serves as a quintessential example. Top executives were embroiled in one of the largest corporate frauds in history, leading to massive financial losses for employees and investors. Yet, the sentences handed down, while significant, were not as severe as might be expected given the scale of the crime. Jeffrey Skilling, the former CEO, received a 24-year sentence, later reduced, which many viewed as inadequate given the devastation caused. Conversely, Martha Stewart's case, involving insider trading, resulted in a five-month prison sentence. Though her crime was far less impactful than Enron's, it highlighted how even minor white-collar offenses can lead to prison time, though often lighter than sentences for violent crimes.

Socio-economic status plays a significant role in the sentencing of white-collar criminals. These offenders often hail from privileged backgrounds, with access to resources that can influence the legal process. High-profile defense teams, connections, and the ability to pay restitution can alter sentencing outcomes, leading to perceptions of bias in the justice system. Societal status can sometimes afford these individuals leniency, as judges may view them as capable of rehabilitation or less likely to reoffend. This contrasts starkly with offenders from less affluent backgrounds, who may not receive the same level of consideration or have similar resources in their defense.

Efforts to address these sentencing disparities have led to legislative reforms aimed at creating more equitable outcomes. The Sentencing Guidelines, established to provide consistency, have been adjusted over the years to better reflect the seriousness of white-collar offenses. However, the U.S. Sentencing Commission has struggled to balance these guidelines with judicial discretion. The landmark Supreme Court decision in United States v. Booker rendered these guidelines advisory rather than mandatory, restoring some discretion to judges. This move aimed to allow for more individualized sentences but has also contributed to variability in outcomes. Reforms continue to evolve, with ongoing debates about the need for stricter penalties and the role of judicial discretion in achieving justice.

The disparities in sentencing for white-collar crime highlight a broader conversation about fairness and accountability in the justice system. While reforms have sought to bridge the gap between different types of offenses, challenges remain in ensuring that sentences reflect the harm caused and the culpability of the offender. As society continues to grapple with these issues, the need for thoughtful consideration and equitable justice becomes ever more apparent.

Juvenile Sentencing: Balancing Reform and Punishment

Juvenile sentencing stands apart in the justice system, reflecting a distinct emphasis on rehabilitation over punishment. The guiding principles of juvenile justice are rooted in the belief that young offenders possess a greater capacity for change. The system aims to correct rather than merely punish, providing opportunities for education, counseling, and community service. This approach acknowledges that adolescents are still developing, both cognitively and emotionally, and that their actions may not fully reflect their potential for future contributions to society. Rehabilitation efforts are designed to address the underlying issues that lead to delinquent behavior, such as family dynamics, peer pressure, and mental health challenges. The focus is on steering juveniles away from a life of crime and toward a productive future.

Landmark cases have significantly shaped the juvenile justice landscape, setting important precedents in how young offenders are treated. A pivotal case is Roper v. Simmons, where the Supreme Court ruled that it is unconstitutional to impose the death penalty on individuals who committed crimes as juveniles. This decision underscored the recognition that juveniles are fundamentally different from adults in terms of culpability and maturity, leading to a reevaluation of the harshest penalties for young offenders. The ruling emphasized the importance of considering age and developmental stage in sentencing, acknowledging that juveniles have a unique potential for growth and rehabilitation. By abolishing the juvenile death penalty, the case reinforced the focus on rehabilitation as a core tenet of juvenile justice, aligning legal practices with psychological and developmental research.

The role of age and maturity in sentencing decisions cannot be overstated. Judges must carefully consider the developmental stage of young offenders when determining appropriate sentences. Adolescents are more impulsive and susceptible to external influences, which can affect their decision-making processes. This understanding is crucial in evaluating their actions and determining the most effective sentencing approach. The justice system seeks to balance accountability with the recognition that young offenders may not fully comprehend the consequences of their actions. This nuanced approach aims to provide sentences that facilitate personal growth, offering offenders the chance to learn from their mistakes and make positive changes in their lives.

Juvenile sentencing has a significant impact on recidivism rates, with the potential to either deter future offenses or inadvertently contribute to a cycle of crime. Programs aimed at reducing juvenile recidivism focus on providing support and resources that address the root causes of delinquent behavior. These initiatives often include mentorship, educational support, and family counseling, helping young offenders build a foundation for a successful future. Research indicates that when juveniles receive appropriate interventions, their likelihood of reoffending decreases significantly. This highlights the importance of tailoring sentencing approaches to the unique needs of each offender, ensuring that they receive the guidance and support necessary to break free from the cycle of crime.

In exploring the complexities of juvenile sentencing, it becomes clear that the justice system must continually adapt to the evolving understanding of adolescent development. By prioritizing rehabilitation and carefully considering the individual circumstances of each young offender, the system seeks to balance the need for accountability with the potential for reform. This approach not only benefits the offenders themselves but also promotes safer communities by reducing recidivism and encouraging positive contributions to society. As the juvenile justice system continues to evolve, it must remain committed to its foundational principles, striving to provide young offenders with the tools and opportunities they need to succeed.

Drug Offenses and the War on Drugs: Sentencing Trends

The landscape of drug-related offenses and their sentencing has been a dynamic field, heavily influenced by policy shifts and public attitudes over the decades. The War on Drugs, initiated in the 1980s, marked a significant era that saw the introduction of mandatory minimum sentences for drug offenses. These laws were designed to impose strict penalties on drug trafficking and possession, reflecting a zero-tolerance stance. Consequently, judges had limited discretion, often leading to harsh sentences that did not account for individual circumstances. The approach aimed to deter drug crimes by ensuring severe consequences, but it soon became apparent that the rigidity of mandatory minimums often led to disproportionate sentences for non-violent offenders. Critics argue that these laws contributed to an overcrowded prison system, with minor offenders serving long sentences alongside hardened criminals.

Case studies of significant drug offenses reveal the impact of these sentencing trends. Large-scale drug trafficking cases, for instance, often result in lengthy prison terms, as exemplified by the case of a notorious drug lord captured after years of evading law enforcement. His sentencing was severe, reflecting the magnitude of his criminal empire and the harm it caused. However, these cases are just one side of the coin. Many individuals, caught in the lower ranks of drug operations, received similar sentences due to mandatory minimums. These cases highlight the challenges of balancing justice with fairness, as sweeping sentencing laws sometimes overlook the nuances of individual involvement and culpability. The result is a justice system that, at times, appears more focused on punishment than rehabilitation.

The impact of drug sentencing on incarceration rates is profound. Statistics reveal that a significant portion of the prison population comprises individuals convicted of drug offenses. This trend has contributed to mass incarceration, straining resources and prompting calls for reform. The high cost of maintaining such a large prison population, coupled with the societal impacts of removing individuals from their communities, underscores the need for alternative approaches. As policymakers grapple with these issues, the conversation has shifted toward finding more effective ways to address drug-related crimes without resorting to excessive incarceration.

In recent years, drug courts have emerged as a promising alternative to traditional sentencing. These specialized courts focus on rehabilitation rather than punishment, aiming to address the root causes of drug-related offenses. Participants in drug court programs receive treatment and support, guided by a structured process that includes regular monitoring and court appearances. The success rates of these programs are encouraging, with participants often showing lower rates of recidivism compared to those who serve traditional sentences. Drug courts emphasize accountability and personal growth, offering offenders a chance to rebuild their lives while reducing the burden on the prison system.

The evolution of sentencing in drug-related offenses reflects a broader shift in the justice system toward more compassionate and effective approaches. As the conversation continues, there is hope that these changes will lead to a more equitable system, where sentences are tailored to fit the individual and the crime, rather than adhering to a one-size-fits-all model.

The Impact of Sentencing in Domestic Violence Cases

Sentencing in domestic violence cases presents unique challenges that require a delicate balance between protecting victims and holding offenders accountable. Unlike other crimes, domestic violence often involves ongoing relationships, making victims' safety a paramount concern. The justice system must navigate the complexities of these relationships, ensuring that sentences do not inadvertently place victims at further risk. Protective orders are a crucial tool, serving as a legal barrier designed to keep offenders away from their victims. These orders are not merely symbolic but also enforceable directives that can include provisions such as no-contact rules and mandatory distance requirements. However, their effectiveness depends on strict enforcement and the willingness of victims to report violations. Judges must weigh these factors carefully, considering the potential for retaliation or continued abuse when crafting sentences.

Case studies of domestic violence sentencing have revealed a range of outcomes, reflecting the complexity of these cases. In some instances, judges have imposed restraining orders alongside jail time to enhance victim protection. For example, a case might involve an offender receiving a sentence that includes both incarceration and a long-term restraining order. This dual approach aims to provide immediate safety while also offering a longer-term solution. In other cases, judges have opted for sentences that focus on rehabilitation, particularly when the offender shows potential for change. This might involve mandated participation in anger management or domestic violence education programs. While these programs aim to address the root causes of abusive behavior, they require careful monitoring to ensure compliance and effectiveness. The variation in sentencing underscores the need for a tailored approach, reflecting the unique circumstances of each case.

Rehabilitation programs play a significant role in the sentencing of domestic violence offenders. These programs are designed to alter behavior and provide offenders with the skills needed to prevent future incidents. Mandated participation in such programs can be part of a sentence, offering a path to rehabilitation while holding offenders accountable for their actions. For these programs to be successful, they must be comprehensive, addressing both the psychological and behavioral aspects of domestic violence. They often include elements such as therapy, education, and community support, all aimed at fostering behavioral change. This approach not only benefits the offender but also contributes to the broader goal of reducing domestic violence in society. However, the success of these programs hinges on consistent implementation and follow-up, ensuring that offenders are genuinely engaged in the process.

Public awareness and advocacy have significantly influenced sentencing practices in domestic violence cases. Increased awareness has led to greater scrutiny of the justice system's handling of these cases, prompting calls for reform. Advocacy groups have played a pivotal role, campaigning for stricter penalties and better support for victims. These efforts have resulted in legislative changes that reflect a deeper understanding of the dynamics of domestic violence. For instance, some jurisdictions have enacted laws that mandate harsher penalties for repeat offenders and those who violate protective orders. These reforms aim to deter offenders and provide victims with greater security. Advocacy groups also work to educate the public and policymakers, highlighting the need for ongoing support and resources for victims. This heightened awareness has shifted public perceptions, leading to a more informed and empathetic approach to domestic violence sentencing.

The impact of sentencing in domestic violence cases extends beyond the courtroom, affecting the lives of victims, offenders, and the community. Therefore, the justice system must continually adapt to the evolving understanding of domestic violence, ensuring that sentences promote safety and accountability. By incorporating protective orders, rehabilitation programs, and public awareness into sentencing practices, the system can better address the complexities of domestic violence. This approach serves the immediate needs of victims and also contributes to the larger goal of preventing future violence. As society continues to grapple with these issues, the need for thoughtful and informed sentencing becomes ever more critical. The lessons learned from these cases inform broader discussions on justice and equity, emphasizing the importance of a compassionate and comprehensive response to crime.

Chapter 4:
Racial Disparities and Bias in Sentencing

Imagine two individuals standing before a judge, charged with similar offenses but emerging from the courtroom with starkly different sentences. This scene is not fictional but a reality that plays out in courtrooms across the United States, reflecting a deeper issue of racial disparities in sentencing. The United States Sentencing Commission's recent report reveals troubling statistics: Black and Hispanic males receive sentences 13.4% and 11.2% longer, respectively, than their White counterparts. Similarly, Hispanic women receive sentences 27.8% longer than White women. These figures underscore a systemic issue where race continues to influence judicial outcomes, leading to questions about fairness and justice.

The root of these disparities can be traced back to historical injustices. The legacy of Jim Crow laws, which enforced racial segregation and disenfranchised African Americans, set a precedent for the racial inequality that permeates the justice system today. The War on Drugs further exacerbated these disparities, as policies disproportionately targeted communities of color. Despite the equal rates of drug use among the races, Black and Hispanic individuals have faced higher rates of arrest and conviction. These historical factors have created a cycle of disadvantage, where racial bias is embedded deep within the structures of the legal system, perpetuating inequity.

Moreover, race and socio-economic status intersect to further compound these disparities. Poverty limits access to quality legal resources, placing minority defendants at a disadvantage. Public defenders, often overworked and under-resourced, cannot provide the robust defense that wealthier defendants might afford. This lack of legal advocacy contributes to longer sentences and higher rates of incarceration for minority groups. The combination of race and socio-economic status creates a dual burden, where individuals are judged not only by their actions but also by the color of their skin and the size of their pockets. This intersectionality highlights the need for a justice system that recognizes and addresses these compounded disadvantages.

Case studies provide concrete examples of how racial disparities manifest in sentencing. One notable case involved a minority defendant charged with a non-violent drug offense. Despite the crime's minor nature, the defendant received a harsh sentence, similar to those given to major drug traffickers. In contrast, a White defendant in a comparable case received a probationary sentence, highlighting the racial bias in sentencing decisions. These cases are not isolated incidents but part of a broader pattern where race influences judicial outcomes. Such disparities call into question the fairness of the justice system and underscore the importance of addressing racial bias in sentencing practices.

Reflection Exercise: Examining Personal Bias

Consider a time when you formed an opinion about someone based on their race or socio-economic status. Reflect on how this bias might have influenced your perception or decisions regarding them. How can recognizing these biases help you advocate for a more equitable justice system? Write your thoughts in a journal, focusing on actions you can take to address and mitigate bias in your daily interactions and broader societal contributions.

Exploring racial disparities in sentencing reveals a complex web of historical, socio-economic, and systemic factors that continue to impact individuals today. Understanding these issues is crucial for those seeking to bring about meaningful reform, whether through policy changes, advocacy, or education. As you engage with these challenges, consider how your role as a student or policymaker can contribute to creating a more just and equitable legal system.

Systemic Bias: The Invisible Hand in Judicial Decisions

Systemic bias permeates every corner of the judicial process, often operating unnoticed yet having profound effects on outcomes. This form of bias does not stem from overt prejudice but rather from embedded institutional policies and practices that give certain groups advantage over others. For example, institutional policies that guide plea bargains and sentencing recommendations can unintentionally favor individuals from specific racial backgrounds, leading to unequal outcomes. Racial profiling is another manifestation of systemic bias, with law enforcement agencies disproportionately targeting minority communities. These practices result in higher arrest rates for minorities, setting the stage for harsher sentencing. The consequences of systemic bias are not confined to individual cases; they reverberate through communities, reinforcing stereotypes and perpetuating cycles of disadvantage.

Institutional racism, deeply rooted in historical contexts, continues to shape sentencing outcomes, influencing how laws are interpreted and applied, often to the detriment of minority communities. Further, judges, guided by precedents and sentencing guidelines, may unconsciously perpetuate systemic racism through their decisions. This is not to imply that all judges act with ill intent; rather, it highlights how systemic racism can permeate even well-intentioned actions. The cumulative effect of these decisions contributes to a justice system that disproportionately penalizes minorities, reflecting broader societal inequities. Such disparities underscore the need for a critical examination of how systemic racism operates within the judiciary and the broader legal framework.

The impact of systemic bias on minority communities is profound and far-reaching. Disproportionate incarceration rates are a clear indicator of how systemic bias manifests in sentencing. Minority groups, particularly Black and Hispanic populations, are incarcerated at rates significantly higher than their White counterparts. This overrepresentation in the prison system exacerbates existing social inequalities, limiting access to employment, education, and housing. The stigma associated with a criminal record further marginalizes these individuals, creating barriers to reintegration and perpetuating cycles of poverty and crime. The broader societal inequalities that stem from systemic bias in sentencing are not merely statistical anomalies but reflect deeper structural issues that require urgent attention.

Real-world examples of systemic bias highlight its pervasive nature and impact. In jurisdictions with high minority populations, sentencing trends reveal stark disparities. For instance, studies have shown that in some areas, minority defendants are more likely to receive longer sentences than their White counterparts for similar offenses. This trend is not isolated but part of a larger pattern that underscores systemic bias. Reports analyzing sentencing data often reveal these disparities, prompting calls for reform and greater accountability within the justice system. Such examples are a critical reminder of the importance of addressing systemic bias to ensure a fair and equitable justice system.

Consider the case of a young Black man charged with a non-violent offense in a predominantly minority community. Despite the minor nature of his crime, he receives a sentence significantly harsher than a White defendant would for a similar offense in a different jurisdiction. This disparity is not merely a reflection of individual judicial discretion but a manifestation of systemic bias. It highlights the need for comprehensive policy changes that address these inequities at their root. By examining these real-world examples, we are reminded of the urgent need to confront systemic bias in all its forms, ensuring true justice for all individuals, regardless of race or background.

The Role of Implicit Bias in the Courtroom

Implicit bias, a term that refers to the subconscious attitudes or stereotypes that affect our understanding, actions, and decisions, is a force that subtly shapes courtroom dynamics. Unlike overt prejudice, implicit bias operates beneath the surface of awareness, influencing behavior in ways that individuals might not consciously recognize. In the courtroom, where fairness and objectivity are paramount, these biases can subtly alter the course of justice. Judges, attorneys, and jurors—all key players in the legal process—are not immune to the influences of implicit bias. For a judge, implicit bias may manifest in decisions about bail, sentencing, or credibility assessments, swaying outcomes despite the intention to remain impartial. When attorneys prepare cases, implicit bias might influence which strategies they employ and how they interpret the demeanor of witnesses and defendants. Jurors, tasked with evaluating evidence and delivering verdicts, may unknowingly allow biases to color their perceptions, leading to decisions that reflect subconscious prejudices rather than facts.

Studies have highlighted the pervasive nature of implicit bias within judicial contexts. Research on judicial awareness has shown that even experienced judges can exhibit biases while ruling. For example, a study revealed that judges with higher levels of awareness about their own biases tend to deliver more balanced decisions, suggesting that acknowledging and understanding implicit bias are crucial steps in mitigating its effects. The challenge lies in recognizing these biases, which often contradict one's conscious beliefs about fairness and equality. Awareness programs aimed at judicial officers can highlight how implicit bias operates, encouraging reflection and self-examination. This understanding can lead to more equitable decisions and a judicial process that aligns more closely with the ideals of justice.

To address implicit bias, the legal community has explored various strategies that can be implemented within courtroom proceedings. Bias training programs for legal professionals have emerged as a foundational step in this journey. Such programs are designed to educate judges, attorneys, and other courtroom personnel about the nature of implicit bias and provide them with tools to identify and counteract its influence. These training sessions often include exercises that reveal personal biases and offer techniques to prevent these biases from affecting decision-making processes. Another innovative approach is implementing blind sentencing reviews, where key identifying information about the defendant is withheld during initial decision-making phases. This method aims to reduce the impact of unconscious biases by focusing on the facts of the case rather than the personal attributes of those involved.

Several case studies provide tangible examples of implicit bias in action, illustrating both its impact and the efforts to mitigate it. Consider a trial where implicit bias was identified and addressed, leading to a review of the sentencing process. In one instance, a defendant from a minority background received a significantly harsher sentence than a White defendant with similar charges. Upon investigation, it was found that the harsher sentence stemmed from unconscious biases that influenced the judge's perception of the defendant's character. Consequently, the court revisited the case, incorporating bias mitigation strategies such as peer review and additional training for the judge. This example highlights the potential for systemic change when implicit bias is acknowledged and addressed, paving the way for a more just legal system.

Case Studies: Race and Sentencing Outcomes

In examining the role of race in sentencing outcomes, certain cases stand out as emblematic of the disparities present within our judicial system. Consider two defendants, one Black and one White, both charged with similar drug offenses. Despite comparable criminal histories and circumstances, the Black defendant receives a sentence nearly double that of his White counterpart. This discrepancy cannot simply be attributed to judicial discretion; it reflects a deeper bias within the system. These case studies highlight the significant role race plays in determining sentencing outcomes, revealing a pattern where minority defendants often face harsher penalties. These disparities are not anomalies but rather symptomatic of systemic issues that pervade the justice system, affecting individuals and communities alike.

Public reaction to such disparities often manifests in protests and media coverage, drawing attention to the injustices faced by minority defendants. In several high-profile cases, public outcry has forced the judicial system to reconsider its practices. Media coverage amplifies these voices, bringing the issue of racial disparities in sentencing to the forefront of public discourse. The case of a young Black man sentenced to an excessive prison term for a minor drug offense is one example. The public backlash was swift and vocal, with protests demanding justice and fairness. This pressure pushed the judicial system to reevaluate the case, demonstrating the power of public sentiment in influencing legal outcomes. The media's role in these instances cannot be understated, as it serves as a catalyst for change, shining a light on injustices that might otherwise remain hidden.

The long-term impact of these racially charged cases extends beyond individual outcomes, prompting shifts in legal practices and policies. Changes in jury selection practices, for instance, have been implemented following notable cases where racial bias was evident.

Courts have become more vigilant in ensuring that juries are diverse and representative, recognizing that a fair trial requires an impartial jury. These changes reflect a growing awareness of the need to address racial biases within the legal system. The shift in jury selection practices is a step toward ensuring that all defendants, regardless of race, receive a fair trial. It also underscores the importance of continuous reform in the pursuit of justice, acknowledging that systemic change is necessary to address deeply rooted biases.

Advocacy and legal interventions have played crucial roles in addressing the disparities highlighted by these cases. Civil rights organizations have been at the forefront of these efforts, challenging unjust sentences and advocating for policy changes. Their involvement has been instrumental in bringing about legal challenges that question the fairness of sentencing practices. In one case, a civil rights group intervened on behalf of a minority defendant, arguing that racial bias influenced the sentencing decision. Their efforts led to a successful appeal, resulting in a reduced sentence and setting a precedent for future cases. Such interventions highlight the power of collective action in challenging systemic injustices and serve as a reminder that while the legal system has its flaws, it also has the capacity for reform and improvement.

Reflecting on these case studies, it becomes apparent that racial disparities in sentencing are not just issues of individual bias but are indicative of broader systemic problems. The judicial reasoning behind these decisions often fails to account for the racial dynamics at play, leading to outcomes that perpetuate inequality. Public reaction and advocacy efforts serve to check the system, pushing for accountability and change. These cases remind us that the fight for justice is ongoing and requires vigilance, awareness, and action from all facets of society. They call for a continued commitment to addressing racial disparities and ensuring that the justice system serves all individuals equitably and fairly.

Strategies for Addressing Racial Inequities in Sentencing

Addressing racial disparities in sentencing demands a multifaceted approach, one that is already underway in various forms. Current strategies aim to mitigate these inequities through education, community support, and systemic reform. Legal education initiatives are at the forefront, striving to instill racial justice awareness in future legal professionals. Moreover, many law schools have integrated courses that focus on racial bias and equity, preparing students to recognize and confront these issues in their careers. By embedding these principles into the curriculum, educational institutions hope to cultivate a generation of lawyers and judges equipped to advocate for fairer legal practices.

Community-based legal aid programs also play a crucial role in reducing racial disparities. These programs provide essential support to individuals who lack the resources to mount an adequate defense. By offering free or low-cost legal services, they help level the playing field for minorities who might otherwise face harsher sentences due to inadequate representation. Such programs often operate at the grassroots level, embedded within communities to ensure accessibility and trust. They not only assist in individual cases but also work to raise awareness about systemic issues, encouraging community involvement in advocacy efforts.

Advocacy groups and grassroots movements have long been champions of racial equity in the justice system. Organizations like the NAACP lead campaigns that raise public awareness and pressure policymakers to enact change. These groups organize protests, lobby legislators, and use media platforms to highlight injustices and advocate for reform. Their efforts have resulted in significant policy shifts and increased public scrutiny of racial bias in sentencing. By mobilizing support across diverse communities, these movements amplify voices that might otherwise go unheard, driving systemic change through collective action.

Innovative approaches are emerging to combat racial inequities. Restorative justice circles, for instance, offer an alternative to traditional sentencing by focusing on healing and reconciliation. These circles bring together offenders, victims, and community members to discuss the impact of the crime and agree on a way forward. By emphasizing dialogue and understanding, restorative justice circles aim to address the root causes of criminal behavior and promote racial equity by involving all stakeholders in the justice process. This approach seeks to not only repair harm but also dismantle the biases that often skew traditional sentencing outcomes.

Case studies of successful interventions provide examples of how targeted efforts can reduce disparities. In one instance, a community-based program focused on providing mentorship and support to young minority offenders showed statistically significant improvements in sentencing equity. Participants were less likely to receive disproportionate sentences compared to those who did not participate in the program. This success was attributed to the program's comprehensive approach, addressing both legal representation and the social factors contributing to criminal behavior. Such programs demonstrate the impact of holistic strategies that consider the broader context of racial disparities, offering a blueprint for similar initiatives.

The path to addressing racial inequities in sentencing is complex and requires persistent effort across multiple domains. Education, community involvement, advocacy, and innovative practices all contribute to a more equitable justice system. As these strategies continue to evolve and expand, they offer a vision of a future where justice is truly blind to race.

Policy Reforms Aimed at Reducing Racial Disparities

In recent years, the legal landscape has seen a concerted effort to tackle the racial disparities ingrained in sentencing practices. Legislative reforms have been pivotal in this endeavor, with the Fair Sentencing Act of 2010 marking a significant milestone. This Act aimed to rectify the disproportionate sentences for crack versus powder cocaine offenses, a disparity that had disproportionately affected Black communities. By reducing the sentencing disparity between these two forms of cocaine, the Act sought to alleviate some of the systemic biases that had plagued the justice system. The impact was immediate, as thousands of inmates became eligible for sentence reductions, highlighting the profound difference legislative changes can make in addressing racial inequities. Yet, while these laws signal progress, they also reveal the complexity of eradicating deep-seated disparities.

However, the path to implementing such reforms is fraught with challenges. Political resistance often emerges as a formidable barrier. Sentencing reform can be a contentious issue, with differing ideologies shaping the debate. Some policymakers fear that reducing sentences could undermine efforts to combat crime, leading to reluctance in embracing change. This resistance is compounded by political climates that prioritize tough-on-crime rhetoric, making it difficult to garner the necessary support for reform. Additionally, navigating the bureaucratic intricacies of enacting new laws requires considerable effort and collaboration among lawmakers, advocacy groups, and the public. These obstacles illustrate the delicate balance between enacting meaningful reform and addressing the concerns of various stakeholders.

Despite these challenges, judicial and prosecutorial discretion offer potential avenues for positive change. Training programs for prosecutors on racial bias represent a crucial step in leveraging discretion effectively. By equipping legal professionals with the skills to recognize and counteract bias, these programs aim to ensure that decisions are fair and informed. Such training emphasizes the importance of evaluating cases based on their merits rather than stereotypes and prejudices. This approach not only fosters greater equity in sentencing but also enhances the credibility of the judicial system. Moreover, empowering judges with the discretion to deviate from mandatory minimums allows for a more individualized approach to sentencing, one that can better account for the unique circumstances of each case.

The potential impact of proposed reforms is both promising and complex. Pilot programs testing new sentencing guidelines offer a glimpse into the future of equitable justice. These programs often focus on reducing mandatory minimums, increasing judicial discretion, and incorporating restorative justice practices. Early assessments suggest that such initiatives can lead to more balanced outcomes, reducing racial disparities in sentencing. However, the feasibility of these reforms hinges on continued support and rigorous evaluation. By analyzing the results of pilot programs, policymakers can identify successful strategies and adapt them for wider implementation. This iterative process ensures that reforms remain responsive to the evolving needs of the justice system.

In conclusion, efforts to address racial disparities in sentencing through policy reform underscore a larger commitment to justice. These reforms represent both a response to past injustices and a proactive approach to shaping a fairer future. Although challenges remain, the ongoing dialogue and legislative action signal a path toward meaningful change. In the next chapter, we will explore ethical and social considerations in sentencing, further highlighting the multifaceted nature of justice.

Chapter 5:
Ethical and Social Considerations

Imagine a small town where nearly every family has felt the impact of incarceration. A father is absent, a mother struggles to make ends meet, and children face the world without the guidance they once had. The ripples of one sentencing decision extend far beyond the walls of a prison, influencing the very fabric of the community. This is not just a story of individuals but of a society grappling with the consequences of its justice system. Sentencing decisions do not occur in isolation; they reverberate through neighborhoods, affecting economic stability, family dynamics, and social cohesion. As you delve into these complexities, consider how these decisions shape the world around you.

The economic impact of sentencing on communities can be profound, stripping neighborhoods of valuable human resources. When a breadwinner is incarcerated, families often face financial strain, leading to reduced spending and economic activity within the community. This depletion can hinder local businesses and diminish community resources, creating a vicious cycle of poverty and dependency. Economic hardship extends beyond immediate families, affecting community-based support networks that rely on collective strength. As families struggle to cope with the absence of a member, the demand for social services increases, stretching already limited resources. These dynamics can weaken community cohesion, as individuals become more isolated and less capable of contributing to collective well-being.

Families of incarcerated individuals face significant emotional and financial challenges and a reshaping of the structure and roles within the household. The absence of a parent or sibling can lead to shifts in family dynamics, where the remaining members must take on new responsibilities. Children, in particular, may experience confusion and distress as they navigate these changes. The loss of a parent due to incarceration often affects a child's sense of security and belonging, leading to behavioral and academic challenges. Furthermore, child welfare and custody issues may arise, as families struggle to maintain stability and continuity. The emotional toll on children can be long lasting, influencing their development and future prospects. This underscores the importance of support systems that address the unique needs of families affected by incarceration.

Social justice in sentencing involves creating equitable practices that reflect the values of fairness and equality. Equitable sentencing practices seek to minimize disparities and ensure that justice is applied consistently across different communities. This concept extends beyond the courtroom, influencing how communities perceive and experience the justice system. Community-led initiatives play a vital role in advocating for equitable reform, mobilizing resources and voices to push for change. These initiatives often focus on raising awareness, providing education, and engaging policymakers in meaningful dialogue. By fostering a collective understanding of justice, communities can work toward a more inclusive and fair system that respects the rights and dignity of all individuals.

Community programs are instrumental in mitigating the negative effects of sentencing, offering support to affected families and fostering resilience. Community reentry programs provide resources and guidance to individuals transitioning from incarceration to society, helping them reintegrate successfully. These programs often include job training, counseling, and housing assistance, addressing the barriers that ex-convicts face. Educational workshops for children of incarcerated parents offer a safe space for these children to learn and grow, providing them with the tools needed to navigate the many challenges they face. These workshops emphasize the importance of education, self-esteem, and resilience, helping children build a foundation for a brighter future. By supporting both individuals and families, community programs contribute to a more supportive and cohesive society.

Reflection Activity: Community Engagement Exercise

Think about your local community and identify any programs or initiatives that support families affected by incarceration. Reflect on how these programs might strengthen community ties and promote social justice. If such initiatives are lacking in your community, consider how you or your peers could contribute to developing supportive networks. Engage with local organizations or policymakers to explore potential collaborations and advocate for change. By taking on an active role, you can help create a community that values inclusivity and resilience.

Restorative Justice: A New Paradigm in Sentencing

Restorative justice represents a shift away from traditional punitive approaches, focusing instead on healing and reconciliation. This approach emphasizes repairing the harm caused by criminal behavior through inclusive processes involving victims, offenders, and the community. The objective is not merely to punish but also to restore relationships and reintegrate offenders into society. At its core, restorative justice seeks to transform the way we think about crime and punishment, helping us to view crime as a violation of people and relationships rather than just a breach of the law. By engaging all stakeholders in dialogue, restorative justice creates opportunities for understanding, accountability, and progress.

Restorative justice can be successfully implemented in various settings, including schools and community mediation programs. In educational environments, restorative justice circles offer a platform for students to discuss conflicts and reach resolutions collaboratively. These circles empower participants to voice their feelings and contribute to finding lasting solutions, fostering a sense of community and mutual respect. In community mediation programs, trained facilitators guide dialogues between victims and offenders, focusing on helping the offender understand the impact of the crime and agreeing on steps to make amends. Such programs have been instrumental in addressing minor offenses and neighborhood disputes, reducing the need for formal legal intervention and promoting harmony within communities.

The benefits of restorative justice are manifold, yet this approach is not without its challenges. One of its primary strengths lies in its ability to reduce recidivism rates. By addressing the root causes of criminal behavior and involving offenders in the resolution process, restorative justice can lead to meaningful behavioral change. Offenders who participate in restorative justice programs often demonstrate higher compliance with restitution and lower rates of reoffending. However, gaining acceptance from traditional justice stakeholders can be difficult, as some of them view restorative justice as too lenient, questioning whether it provides adequate deterrence and punishment. This skepticism often poses a barrier to a broader implementation of restorative justice, requiring continuous efforts to educate and demonstrate the efficacy of these practices.

A central component of restorative justice is the victim–offender dialogue, which plays a crucial role in the healing process. These dialogues allow victims to express the emotional and practical impact of the crime directly to the offender, fostering empathy and understanding. For victims, this interaction can be empowering, providing a sense of closure and control over the justice process. Offenders, in turn, gain insight into the consequences of their actions, which can be a powerful catalyst for change. Case studies of victim–

offender reconciliation highlight the positive outcomes of these dialogues. In one instance, a burglary victim and the offender engaged in a mediated dialogue, where the offender apologized and agreed to perform community service to make amends. This process not only helped the victim regain a sense of safety but also motivated the offender to pursue a crime-free life.

The impact of these dialogues on victims' emotional recovery is significant, offering them a path to healing that traditional sentencing often lacks. While a conventional court process might focus solely on punishment, restorative justice provides room for victims to be heard and acknowledged. This recognition can be instrumental in rebuilding trust and confidence in the justice system. Additionally, the collaborative nature of restorative justice encourages community involvement, fostering a sense of collective responsibility for addressing crime and its consequences. By prioritizing relationships and community well-being, restorative justice challenges us to rethink how we define and achieve justice.

Media Representation and Public Perception of Sentencing

In a world where news cycles move at lightning speed, the media wields immense power in shaping the public's perception of sentencing. Imagine a headline screaming about a lenient sentence handed down to a high-profile defendant. It's the kind of story that invites clicks and fuels discussions, yet often lacks the nuance needed to understand the complexities of the case. Sensationalism in crime reporting isn't new, but its influence has grown as media outlets compete for attention. This style of reporting tends to emphasize drama over detail, painting a picture that may not accurately reflect the judicial process. The result is a skewed public understanding of how sentences are determined, often leading to misconceptions and misplaced outrage.

The media's role in perpetuating bias and stereotypes further complicates the narrative. Racial bias is a persistent issue, with studies indicating that media coverage often portrays minority defendants more negatively than their White counterparts. This bias can influence public opinion, fostering stereotypes that equate race with criminality. A case study illustrates how a Black defendant receives harsher media scrutiny than a White defendant facing similar charges, reinforcing harmful stereotypes. Such portrayals not only affect public perception but can also seep into policy discussions, where lawmakers may feel pressured to respond to the narrative rather than to facts. When the media focuses on the sensational aspects of a case, critical elements like the defendant's background or mitigating circumstances are often overshadowed, leading to an incomplete picture of justice.

The consequences of media influence extend beyond public opinion, shaping policy-making and judicial decisions. When a story captures the public's attention, it often leads to outcry, prompting legislators to act. This has been evident in the aftermath of several high-profile cases where perceived injustices led to calls for tougher sentencing laws. While public engagement in justice reform is essential, policy changes driven by media narratives rather than data can have unintended consequences. Reactionary measures may prioritize appeasing public sentiment over addressing systemic issues in the justice system, leading to laws that do not necessarily enhance fairness or justice. This dynamic underscores the need for thoughtful discourse informed by comprehensive understanding rather than sensational headlines.

Promoting accurate media representation of sentencing is crucial for fostering informed public discussions. Collaboration between media and legal experts can help bridge the gap between sensational reporting and nuanced analysis. Legal professionals can provide context and clarity, helping journalists present a balanced view of complex cases. This collaboration would benefit both the media and public, offering insights that are often missed in the media's rush to publish. Organizing workshops and training sessions for journalists on legal reporting can enhance their understanding of the justice system, improving the quality of their coverage. Encouraging a move away from sensationalism toward comprehensive storytelling will allow audiences engage more deeply with the issues at hand.

Media Literacy Exercise: Critical Analysis

As you encounter news stories about criminal sentencing, take a moment to analyze the coverage critically. Consider the language used and the perspectives represented. Are there racial undertones? Is the focus on sensational details rather than the broader context? Reflect on how the story might shape your perception of justice and whether it encourages a deeper understanding of the issues involved. Engaging with the media critically empowers you to see beyond the headlines and consider the complexities of sentencing. By fostering media literacy, you can contribute to more informed discussions about justice and policy reform.

Ethical Dilemmas in Judicial Decision-Making

In the solitude of their chambers, judges often grapple with ethical dilemmas that test their professional obligations and personal values. Sentencing, a critical aspect of their role, brings these challenges to bear. Judges must navigate a complex moral landscape where the law's demands may conflict with their own ethical beliefs. Consider a case where the law mandates a harsh sentence for a minor drug offense. The judge may personally believe in leniency and rehabilitation but is bound by legal precedent and guidelines. This conflict between legal obligations and personal ethics is a constant in their decision-making, requiring careful balancing. Judges must weigh the scales of justice with the knowledge that their decisions will have profound effects on the lives of those before them as well as on the broader community.

Ethical frameworks and guidelines help judges navigate these dilemmas, helping them maintain integrity and fairness. Judicial codes of conduct, such as the Model Code of Judicial Conduct in the United States, outline standards for ethical behavior and decision-making. These codes emphasize principles like impartiality, independence, and integrity, guiding judges in resolving ethical conflicts. They serve as a compass, reminding judges of their duty to apply the law consistently while respecting individual rights. However, codes of conduct cannot anticipate every scenario, leaving judges to rely on their judgment when faced with unprecedented situations. In such cases, ethical guidelines provide a framework, but the ultimate responsibility to interpret and apply these principles in the context of each unique case lies with the judge.

Notable cases of ethical conflict in sentencing illustrate the challenges judges face. One prominent example involved a judge known for advocating rehabilitation over incarceration. In a high-profile case, he recused himself, citing a personal connection to the defendant that could compromise his impartiality. This decision highlights the ethical dilemma of maintaining objectivity while acknowledging personal biases. Another case saw a judge struggle with sentencing a juvenile offender under mandatory minimum laws, which conflicted with her belief in the potential for rehabilitation. These cases underscore the importance of ethical awareness and the courage required to uphold integrity in the face of challenging decisions.

Strategies for navigating ethical dilemmas in judicial roles are essential for maintaining ethical integrity. Peer consultation is one effective approach, allowing judges to discuss complex cases with colleagues who can offer diverse perspectives and support. These discussions can illuminate blind spots and provide reassurance, helping judges reach ethical decisions. Ethical review boards also play a crucial role, offering judges guidance and oversight in particularly challenging cases. By reviewing decisions and providing feedback, these boards help judges align their actions with ethical standards. Regular training and education on emerging ethical issues further equip judges to handle the evolving challenges of their roles, fostering a culture of ethical reflection and continuous improvement.

Judges, as arbiters of justice, wield significant power and responsibility. Their decisions often shape lives and communities, making ethical integrity vital for them. Understanding the ethical dilemmas judges face is crucial for anyone interested in the justice system, be it a student aspiring to a legal career or a policymaker seeking to influence judicial practices. By exploring these challenges and the strategies used to address them, we gain insight into the complexities of judicial decision-making and the importance of maintaining ethical standards in the pursuit of justice.

Sentencing and Mental Health: A Dual Challenge

In the courtroom, where justice is sought and sentences are handed down, the presence of mental health issues in defendants adds a layer of complexity to an already nuanced process. Mental health disorders can affect behavior and decision-making, complicating the determination of culpability and appropriate sentencing. Identifying these disorders in defendants requires careful assessment, as mental health conditions can manifest in various ways, influencing both the crime committed and the offender's ability to participate in their defense. Accurate identification allows the legal system to distinguish between criminal intent and actions driven by mental illness, highlighting the importance of nuanced evaluations in the sentencing process.

Mental health assessments play a pivotal role in courts, providing a foundation for informed sentencing decisions. Psychological evaluations are integral to understanding a defendant's mental state, offering insights into how their condition might have influenced their actions. These assessments require expertise and sensitivity, as they delve into complex psychological landscapes to present a clear picture to the court. The results can guide judges in tailoring sentences that consider the defendant's mental health needs, potentially leading to alternative sentencing options designed to address these needs rather than defaulting to incarceration. This approach aligns with a more rehabilitative vision of justice, one that sees beyond the crime to the individual and their potential for change.

Alternative sentencing options for mentally ill offenders provide pathways that focus on treatment and rehabilitation rather than punishment. Mental health courts have emerged as specialized forums that emphasize therapeutic jurisprudence, aiming to connect defendants with mental health resources and support services. These courts operate with a multidisciplinary team approach, bringing together judges, attorneys, mental health professionals, and social workers to create comprehensive care plans. The effectiveness of mental health courts lies in their ability to reduce recidivism by addressing the underlying issues contributing to criminal behavior. Rehabilitation-focused sentencing options, such as mandated therapy and community-based treatment programs, offer additional avenues for supporting mentally ill offenders. These alternatives prioritize stabilization and recovery, aiming to reduce offenders' future interactions with the criminal justice system.

Incarceration poses significant risks to inmates' mental health, often exacerbating already existing conditions or precipitating new ones. The prison environment, characterized by isolation, lack of privacy, and limited access to mental health care, can have detrimental effects on individuals with mental illnesses. Solitary confinement, in particular, is notorious for its severe psychological impact, leading to increased anxiety, depression, and even psychosis. The stress of imprisonment can intensify symptoms, making rehabilitation more challenging and undermining efforts to prepare inmates for successful reintegration into society. These realities underscore the need for a justice system that recognizes the complex interplay between mental health and criminal behavior, advocating for approaches that prioritize treatment and support over punitive measures.

Mental health and sentencing intersect in ways that demand a more compassionate and informed approach to justice. By acknowledging the role of mental health in criminal behavior, the legal system can craft responses that are not only fair but also effective in promoting the long-term well-being of individuals and communities. This perspective challenges traditional notions of punishment, urging a shift toward solutions that address the root causes of crime. This way, the justice system can better serve its purpose, fostering an environment where rehabilitation and recovery are possible and where individuals are given the opportunity to rebuild their lives with dignity and support.

Exploring the Human Cost of Incarceration

The experience of incarceration extends far beyond the physical confines of a prison cell, leaving lasting impressions on individuals and the society. One of the most significant consequences is the loss of human capital and productivity. When individuals are removed from the workforce, communities lose their contributions, both economic and social. This loss can hinder local economies, as the skills and labor of the incarcerated are no longer available to bolster industries or support families. Moreover, the stigma associated with having a criminal record can be a barrier to reentry into the job market, creating a cycle where former inmates struggle to find employment, exacerbating poverty and social inequality.

The societal stigma faced by those who have served time is another profound issue. Formerly incarcerated individuals often encounter prejudice and discrimination in their professional and personal lives. This stigma can manifest in various ways, from difficulties in securing housing to challenges in rebuilding relationships. Society's perception of ex-offenders as perpetual lawbreakers often hinders their reintegration, leading to isolation and marginalization. This societal view not only impacts these individuals but also affects their families and communities, creating an environment where recidivism becomes more likely due to lack of support and opportunities.

Incarceration also takes a heavy emotional and psychological toll on inmates, compounding the challenges they face. The prison environment, characterized by isolation and lack of support, can exacerbate mental health issues or lead to new ones. The absence of meaningful social interactions, combined with the stress of confinement, often leads to feelings of anxiety, depression, and hopelessness. These conditions make it difficult for inmates to maintain their mental health, and without appropriate support, these challenges can persist long after release. This mental strain affects the individual as well as their ability to reintegrate into society, impacting their families and communities.

Long-term incarceration compounds these issues, presenting unique challenges for reintegration. Extended sentences can sever ties with family and friends, making ex-offenders' transition back into society daunting. Inmates may find that the world has moved on without them, making it difficult for them to reconnect with loved ones or find their place within their communities. This disconnection can lead to strained relationships, further isolating the individual and hindering their ability to reintegrate successfully. The long-term effects on personal relationships are significant, affecting the very fabric of family and community life and making the path to rehabilitation more challenging.

To address these challenges, various initiatives aimed at reducing the human cost of incarceration have emerged. Educational and vocational training programs within prisons offer inmates the opportunity to develop new skills in preparation for life after release. These programs focus on equipping inmates with the knowledge and experience needed to secure employment, thus reducing the likelihood of reoffending. By equipping them with tangible skills and fostering a sense of purpose, these initiatives play a crucial role in promoting successful reintegration. Additionally, support services for reintegration, such as counseling and job placement assistance, help bridge the gap between incarceration and community life. These services address the practical and emotional needs of ex-offenders, offering them guidance and support as they navigate the complexities of reentry.

Considering the broader human impact of incarceration, it becomes clear that the justice system must evolve to address these challenges. By focusing on rehabilitation and support, rather than merely punishment, we can work toward creating a system that values human potential and fosters societal well-being. The next chapter will explore comparative global sentencing practices, examining innovative approaches that other countries have implemented to balance justice with humanity.

Chapter 6:
The Role of the Media and
Public Perception

In a bustling city, a high-stakes courtroom drama unfolds, not within the halls of justice but on a silver screen. The audience watches as the charismatic lawyer delivers a passionate closing argument, the camera capturing every dramatic pause and rhetorical flourish. The judge, stern and wise, delivers a verdict that resonates with the viewers as the theme music rises. This scene, though fictional, profoundly impacts how many perceive the criminal justice system. Popular media, through films and television, plays a crucial role in shaping our understanding of legal proceedings, including sentencing. As gatekeepers of information, media narratives frame how we view justice, influencing both our expectations and beliefs.

Films and television often portray judges and lawyers through a lens of stereotypes. Judges are depicted as either stern arbiters of justice or sympathetic figures swayed by compelling arguments. Lawyers, in contrast, are often portrayed as either noble defenders of the innocent or cunning manipulators of the law. Such portrayals simplify complex roles, reducing them to familiar caricatures that audiences easily recognize. These stereotypes create a distorted view of the legal profession, where real-life complexities and ethical dilemmas are overshadowed by dramatization. The reality is far more nuanced, with judges and lawyers navigating intricate legal frameworks while attempting to balance ethical considerations with the pursuit of justice.

Courtroom proceedings in media are dramatized to heighten excitement and engage viewers. Legal dramas condense long trials into neatly packaged narratives that fit within an episode or film. This compression often leads to oversimplification, where intricate legal arguments are distilled into quick exchanges and dramatic revelations.

In reality, trials involve meticulous examination of evidence, procedural rules, and deliberations that rarely reach cinematic levels of drama. The dramatization serves to entertain but risks misleading audiences about the true nature of legal processes. By focusing on sensational elements, these narratives often obscure the painstaking work involved in real-world legal proceedings.

Fictional narratives exert a powerful influence on real-world understanding, shaping the public's expectations about justice. Legal dramas, with their engaging storylines, leave viewers with unrealistic expectations about the speed and decisiveness of the justice system. The portrayal of swift justice, where cases are resolved with clear outcomes, contrasts sharply with the often lengthy and complex nature of actual legal proceedings. This disparity fosters misconceptions about the efficiency and fairness of the system, leading to frustration when reality does not align with dramatized portrayals. Such narratives can also affect beliefs about sentencing, where the punishment may appear either too lenient or excessively harsh based on selective storytelling.

Common themes and tropes in media narratives further shape audience understanding. Crime stories frequently adopt a "good vs. evil" framework, where clear distinctions are drawn between protagonists and antagonists. This binary perspective simplifies the moral complexities inherent in legal cases, where shades of gray often prevail. The portrayal of crime as a battle between good and evil reinforces stereotypes and may perpetuate biases. By presenting crime in such stark terms, media narratives influence how audiences perceive culpability and the appropriateness of sentencing. This reductive approach can lead to skewed perceptions, where justice is seen as a straightforward dichotomy rather than a nuanced balancing act.

The media holds the potential to both educate and misinform, serving as a double-edged sword in shaping informed citizenship. On one hand, educational documentaries about the justice system offer valuable insights, providing viewers with a deeper understanding of legal processes and societal implications. These programs can demystify complex legal concepts, fostering a more informed public discourse. On the other hand, sensationalized portrayals can perpetuate myths and reinforce misconceptions. The challenge lies in discerning fact from fiction and recognizing the limitations of media as a source of information. By critically engaging with media content, audiences can navigate the fine line between entertainment and education, developing a balanced perspective on justice.

Reflection Section: Explore Your Perceptions

Reflect on a recent film or TV show you saw that featured a legal storyline. Consider how its portrayal of judges, lawyers, and courtroom proceedings influenced your understanding of the justice system. Did the narrative align with what you know about real-world legal processes? How might these depictions shape your perceptions of fairness and justice?

The role of media in shaping public perception of sentencing and the justice system is profound. By examining media narratives, we gain insight into how storytelling influences beliefs and expectations, highlighting the importance of critical engagement with the stories that captivate us.

Media Bias and Its Impact on Public Sentiment

Media bias in crime reporting is a pervasive force that shapes how crime and sentencing are perceived by the public. This bias manifests in various ways, from the selective coverage of crime stories to the language and framing choices used in reports. Selective coverage often highlights certain types of crimes or focuses disproportionately on crimes committed by particular demographic groups, skewing public perception. For instance, crimes involving minority suspects may receive more sensationalized coverage, reinforcing stereotypes and fear. This selective focus can lead to an overestimation of crime rates and a warped view of who is committing these crimes. Language plays a crucial role too; words like "thug" and "gang member" carry connotations that can shape viewers' perceptions, often without them realizing it. Such framing can lead to the public developing skewed views on who is most likely to commit crimes and who deserves harsher sentencing.

Sensationalism in crime reporting further distorts public understanding and reactions. Headlines that scream of violent acts grab attention, but they also exaggerate the prevalence of such crimes. This approach prioritizes shock value over factual reporting, leading to a heightened sense of fear and urgency among the public. Sensational stories about violent crimes are more likely to be shared and discussed, creating a feedback loop that amplifies public concern and often leads to calls for tougher sentencing laws. This cycle can distort societal priorities, making it seem as if violent crime is rampant when, in reality, statistics might show a different picture. The result is a public that may push for policies based on fear rather than facts, influencing legislators who feel pressured to respond to constituents' concerns.

The ownership structures of media outlets significantly influence reporting priorities and biases. Large corporations often own multiple media platforms, and their interests can subtly guide the narratives that are prioritized. Corporate interests might lead to an underreporting of crimes that don't align with their agenda or an overemphasis of stories that do. This influence can skew public perception, as the stories that reach the audience are filtered through a corporate lens. Such bias can result in a media landscape where certain crimes are either magnified or diminished based on factors unrelated to their actual impact on society. This disparity in coverage can lead to a misinformed public, unaware of the nuances and breadth of crime and sentencing issues.

To navigate the complex landscape of media bias, audiences must equip themselves with tools to critically assess media content. Media literacy programs are invaluable in this regard, teaching individuals how to discern fact from fiction, recognize bias, and understand the techniques used in news production. These programs encourage critical thinking and skepticism, empowering individuals to question the narratives presented to them. Fact-checking initiatives also play a key role, providing resources that verify the accuracy of reported information. By consulting these sources, audiences can cross-reference news stories, ensuring that they are not accepting biased or incomplete narratives at face value. These strategies are crucial for fostering an informed public that can engage with crime and sentencing issues thoughtfully and critically.

How Public Perception Shapes Sentencing Policies

In today's interconnected world, public opinion exerts significant influence over policy-making, particularly in the realm of criminal sentencing. The relationship between what the public thinks and how laws are shaped is dynamic and complex. Public opinion polls often serve as a barometer for lawmakers, reflecting societal attitudes toward crime and punishment. For example, when polls indicate strong support for harsher penalties for certain offenses, legislators may feel compelled to act. This responsiveness can be seen as a democratic strength, as them ensuring that the justice system reflects the will of the people. However, it also raises questions about the role of informed decision-making in policy creation. When public sentiment shifts toward reform, as seen in recent calls for more equitable sentencing, lawmakers may prioritize these changes to align with evolving societal values.

The media plays a crucial role in shaping public perception, thereby influencing legislative priorities. High-profile cases, often sensationalized by the media, can create public pressure, which politicians find hard to ignore. The coverage of such cases can lead to swift legislative action, sometimes resulting in new laws and reforms. For instance, the intense media spotlight on certain violent crimes has prompted legislative bodies to enact stricter sentencing laws. While this media-fueled pressure can lead to necessary reforms, it also poses the risk of influencing the creation of reactionary policies that may not be thoroughly considered. Laws enacted in response to public outcry, such as mandatory minimum sentences, might address immediate concerns but can later reveal unintended consequences, like increased incarceration rates without corresponding benefits in crime reduction.

The influence of public opinion on sentencing policies can be illustrated through specific examples. For instance, the "three-strike" laws, which mandate severe sentences for repeat offenders, emerged largely due to public demand for tougher crime measures. These laws gained momentum following media campaigns that highlighted cases where habitual offenders committed serious crimes. While these policies aimed to deter repeat offenses, they also sparked debates about fairness and proportionality in sentencing. Critics argue that such laws contribute to prison overcrowding and disproportionately affect marginalized communities. This example underscores the role of public perception in shaping policies, highlighting the delicate balance between responding to societal demands and ensuring just legal frameworks.

The interplay between public sentiment and policy-making presents both opportunities and challenges. On one hand, aligning laws with public opinion can enhance their legitimacy and acceptance. On the other hand, it can lead to reactionary policies that prioritize popular demands over informed decision-making. The challenge lies in balancing responsiveness with governance that is based on evidence and expert insights. Policymakers must navigate this landscape carefully, ensuring that reforms are not only popular but also effective and equitable. They must weigh the benefits of catering to public sentiment against the potential risks of enacting policies that may later prove flawed or unjust.

In navigating this landscape, policymakers can benefit from a nuanced understanding of public opinion and its drivers. The media's role in shaping perceptions, particularly through its portrayal of crime and justice issues, cannot be underestimated. As public sentiment continues to evolve, driven by both media narratives and changing societal values, the task of crafting sentencing policies that are fair, effective, and reflective of contemporary norms remains a complex and ongoing challenge.

The Role of Advocacy and Public Campaigns in Reform

In today's digital age, advocacy groups have developed sophisticated strategies to influence public opinion and drive policy change. One of the most potent tools in their arsenal is social media. Platforms like Twitter, Facebook, and Instagram enable these organizations to reach vast audiences rapidly, mobilizing support for their causes. By crafting compelling narratives and using hashtags, advocacy groups can create viral campaigns that capture public attention. These campaigns often focus on highlighting injustices within the sentencing system, using real-life stories to evoke empathy and drive engagement. The immediacy and reach of social media allow these groups to bypass traditional media gatekeepers, communicating directly with the public and shaping perceptions in real-time.

Public awareness campaigns play a crucial role in educating the public about sentencing issues. These campaigns often employ a combination of traditional media (such as television and radio ads) and digital content to disseminate their message. The goal is to raise awareness about specific sentencing practices, such as mandatory minimums, and their impact on individuals and communities. By presenting clear, accessible information, these campaigns aim to demystify complex legal issues, empowering the public to engage with policy debates. Through targeted messaging, advocacy groups can shift public discourse, creating a groundswell of support for reform initiatives that might otherwise remain on the political fringe.

Grassroots movements are another vital component of advocacy efforts, providing a bottom-up approach to reform. These movements often begin at the local level, driven by individuals and community groups passionate about change. Community-driven reform campaigns can be particularly effective, as they engage citizens directly affected by sentencing policies. By organizing rallies, town hall meetings, and other public events, these movements raise awareness and foster community involvement. Successful grassroots advocacy can bring national attention to local issues, influencing broader reform initiatives. Examples of successful grassroots efforts include the campaigns that led to the repeal of harsh sentencing laws and the establishment of alternative sentencing programs.

Celebrity endorsements can amplify the reach and impact of advocacy campaigns. Public figures with large followings can lend their voices to causes, drawing media attention and highlighting issues that might otherwise go unnoticed. Celebrities can use their platforms to educate their audiences, providing a bridge between advocacy groups and the public. Campaigns backed by celebrities often gain traction quickly, as their involvement brings credibility and visibility. For instance, high-profile figures have supported sentencing reform efforts, calling for changes to draconian laws and advocating for more equitable justice practices. By leveraging their influence, celebrities can help shift public opinion and spur policymakers into action.

Several advocacy campaigns have successfully led to tangible policy changes and increased public awareness. For example, campaigns focused on sentencing reform have sparked legislative hearings and prompted lawmakers to reconsider outdated practices. These campaigns often utilize a combination of storytelling, data, and strategic partnerships to build a compelling case for change. One notable example is the campaign to end juvenile life without parole, which gained momentum through advocacy efforts and resulted in significant legal shifts across multiple states. Another campaign, aimed at reducing mandatory minimum sentences for non-violent drug offenses, highlighted the personal stories of those affected and successfully lobbied for legislative reform. These case studies demonstrate the power of advocacy in driving meaningful change and underscore the importance of public involvement in the reform process.

Case Studies: Media Influence in High-Profile Cases

In the annals of media history, few trials have garnered as much attention and scrutiny as the O.J. Simpson trial. The case, which unfolded in the mid-1990s, became a cultural phenomenon, dominating headlines and capturing the public's imagination. The trial's media coverage was nothing short of sensational, with 24-hour news cycles dedicated to every twist and turn. As cameras rolled both inside and outside the courtroom, the case became a spectacle, a real-life drama that blurred the lines between news and entertainment. This intense media attention shaped public perception, turning the trial into a referendum on race, celebrity, and the American justice system.

Different media outlets played distinct roles in shaping the narrative of the O.J. Simpson case. Newspapers, with their detailed reporting and in-depth analysis, provided a platform for public discourse, examining the implications of the trial beyond the courtroom. In contrast, television coverage focused on the visual and emotional aspects, often emphasizing courtroom drama and the personalities involved. This duality in coverage created a multifaceted narrative that influenced public opinion in complex ways. The sensationalism inherent in television reporting, with its emphasis on sound bites and dramatic moments, often overshadowed the nuanced analysis found in print media. This disparity in coverage highlighted the media's power to frame narratives, affecting how audiences interpreted the trial's proceedings and outcomes.

The impact of media coverage on the involved parties was profound. For defendants, such as Simpson, the constant media scrutiny added an additional layer of pressure, complicating their legal strategies and public personas. The relentless spotlight magnified every gesture and word, creating a parallel trial in the court of public opinion. The victims and their families also found themselves thrust into the limelight, their grief and suffering laid bare for the world to see. This exposure led to emotional distress, as private pain was transformed into public spectacle. The intense media focus also had broader societal implications, influencing public attitudes toward the justice system and shaping perceptions of fairness and bias.

The long-term implications of media coverage on legal practices are significant. The O.J. Simpson trial, for instance, prompted changes in courtroom media access policies. The case demonstrated the potential for media presence to disrupt proceedings, leading to debates about the appropriateness of cameras in courtrooms. In response, some jurisdictions implemented stricter guidelines, balancing transparency with the need to maintain judicial decorum. The trial also sparked discussions about the media's role in shaping justice-related narratives, highlighting the need for ethical guidelines to prevent sensationalism from overshadowing substantive reporting. These developments underscore the evolving relationship between media and the justice system, as both seek to navigate the complex interplay of information, perception, and truth.

Crafting Effective Media Strategies for Sentencing Advocacy

In the realm of advocacy, crafting an effective media strategy is paramount to capturing attention and driving change. At the heart of a successful campaign lies the ability to develop clear and compelling messages that resonate with the target audience. Advocates must distill complex issues into digestible narratives that convey urgency and relevance. This involves identifying the core message that aligns with the values and concerns of the audience, ensuring that it is both relatable and motivating. Once the message is crafted, it becomes essential to identify and target key media outlets that can amplify it. Different outlets have varying reach and influence, so selecting the right platforms is crucial. Whether it's mainstream news channels, influential blogs, or niche publications, the goal is to place the message where it will have maximum impact.

Digital media has revolutionized advocacy efforts, providing tools and platforms that were unimaginable just a decade ago. With the click of a button, advocates can now reach global audiences, transcending geographical and social boundaries. Viral content, in particular, has the power to raise awareness rapidly, often reaching millions within hours. By creating shareable videos or infographics, advocates can engage audiences in ways that traditional media cannot. Online petitions have also emerged as a potent tool in advocacy, allowing individuals to express support for causes and demand action from policymakers. These petitions can galvanize public opinion, showcasing widespread support and putting pressure on decision-makers. The digital landscape thus provides a dynamic arena for advocates to influence public discourse and policy.

Storytelling serves as a cornerstone of effective advocacy, tapping into the human experience to drive engagement and empathy. Personal stories can transcend statistics, giving a face to the issues at hand. When audiences connect emotionally with narratives, they are more likely to swing into action. Case studies of narrative-driven campaigns underscore the power of storytelling in advocacy. For example, campaigns that highlight the personal experiences of those affected by harsh sentencing laws can evoke empathy and outrage, prompting calls for change. By weaving together personal narratives and broader policy critiques, advocates can create compelling arguments that resonate with the public on both emotional and intellectual levels.

Advocates require a strategic approach to engage with the media, one that involves building relationships with media professionals and effectively managing media relations. Establishing rapport with journalists can lead to more favorable coverage and increased visibility for advocacy efforts. Advocates must take the time to understand the interests and beats of journalists, offering them stories that align with their coverage areas. Crafting press releases and media kits is another critical component, providing journalists with the information they need to cover stories accurately and compellingly. Press releases should be concise and newsworthy, highlighting the most important aspects of a campaign. Media kits can include background information, statistics, and quotes, ensuring that journalists have all the resources necessary to produce informed and engaging content.

As we consider the role of media in shaping public perception of sentencing, it becomes clear that advocacy strategies must be as dynamic and adaptable as the media landscape itself. By leveraging clear messaging, digital tools, storytelling, and media relations, advocates can effectively influence public discourse and drive meaningful change. This chapter has explored these strategies in detail, providing insights into how advocates can harness the power of media to advance their causes. As we move forward, the challenge will be to continue adapting to an ever-evolving media environment, ensuring that advocacy remains impactful and relevant in the pursuit of justice and reform.

Chapter 7:
Comparative Global Sentencing Practices

Imagine a courtroom where the fate of a defendant hinges on the crime committed as well as on the cultural, legal, and political backdrop of the country in which the trial is being held. Consider the contrast between a courtroom in the United States, where determinate sentencing with structured guidelines often prevails, and one in Argentina, where indeterminate sentencing allows for more judicial discretion and potential early release based on rehabilitation. This diversity in sentencing practices reflects the complexity of justice systems worldwide, shaped by varied historical and political contexts that influence how societies perceive crime and punishment.

Globally, countries employ different legal systems that impact sentencing approaches. In common law countries like the United States and United Kingdom, precedents from previous judicial decisions play a significant role in shaping outcomes. Judges have more room to interpret laws, leading to a system where past cases guide future decisions. In contrast, civil law countries such as France and Germany rely on comprehensive legal codes that dictate sentencing procedures with less room for judicial interpretation. Here, the law itself is more prescriptive, aiming for consistency and predictability. These differences highlight how foundational legal traditions can shape the justice process, affecting everything from trial procedures to the severity of sentences.

Sentencing philosophies also diverge across the globe, often reflecting deeper societal values. For instance, retributive justice, which focuses on punishment proportionate to the crime, is prevalent in many Western legal systems, emphasizing deterrence and accountability and viewing incarceration as a necessary response to wrongdoing. On the other hand, rehabilitative justice, favored in countries like Norway, prioritizes the reintegration of offenders into society and views crime as a symptom of social or personal issues that need addressing, with a focus on education and therapy rather than punishment. These philosophical differences underscore how societies choose to address crime, balancing between punitive measures and rehabilitative goals.

A nation's history and political climate are crucial in shaping its sentencing practices. In post-colonial African countries, for example, justice systems often blend traditional practices with imported legal frameworks, creating a hybrid approach that seeks to honor indigenous customs while adhering to modern legal standards. In contrast, Eastern European countries with communist legacies may retain elements of centralized control within their justice systems, reflecting historical priorities of state control and uniformity. These historical influences are evident in sentencing approaches, where political ideologies and cultural traditions intersect in the courtroom.

Consider Japan, where the justice system incorporates elements of restorative justice. Here, the emphasis is on reconciliation and community harmony. Victims participate actively in proceedings, and prosecutors have discretion to suspend prosecutions for offenders showing genuine remorse. This approach reflects deep-rooted cultural values of harmony and societal balance. In stark contrast, Saudi Arabia's use of corporal punishment reflects a different set of cultural and religious values, emphasizing deterrence and adherence to religious law. These examples illustrate the wide spectrum of sentencing practices and highlight how cultural context can lead to vastly different approaches to justice.

Reflection Section: Diverse Perspectives

Reflect on how your own cultural background and legal system might have shaped your views on sentencing. Consider how different approaches, such as retributive and rehabilitative justice, align with your values and how they influence your perception of what constitutes a fair and effective justice system.

By examining these global practices, we gain insight into the diverse ways societies navigate the complex issues of crime and punishment, revealing the deep connections between legal systems and the cultural, historical, and political landscapes in which they operate.

Lessons from Scandinavia: Rehabilitation Over Punishment

Imagine a prison where the walls do not confine but instead support growth and change. This is the essence of the Scandinavian model, particularly in Norway, where rehabilitation takes precedence over punishment. The philosophy underpinning this model is simple yet profound: treat individuals with dignity, focus on their potential for change, and prepare them for reintegration into society. In this system, open prisons are common, with inmates allowed to live in conditions that closely resemble normal life. They have access to education, vocational training, and therapeutic programs aimed at addressing the root causes of their criminal behavior. The goal is clear: to turn prisons into places of healing rather than punishment.

The effectiveness of this rehabilitative approach is evidenced by Norway's low recidivism rates. Statistics reveal that within two years of release, only about 20% of former inmates reoffend, which is much lower than the rates in countries with more punitive systems. This success is not just a reflection of humane prison conditions but also of a broader societal commitment to rehabilitation. Norway's focus on rehabilitation also extends to its economic sphere, as former prisoners experience a 40% increase in employment rates post-release, which is crucial because it reduces the likelihood of reoffending and supports overall societal safety. The system's success is a testament to the fact that when individuals are given the right tools, they often will succeed.

Cultural and societal factors play a significant role in supporting these rehabilitative practices. Scandinavians generally place a high level of trust in their justice system, believing that it functions fairly and effectively. This trust is crucial, as it fosters an environment where rehabilitation thrives. Scandinavian countries also provide robust social welfare support, ensuring that those who have served time have access to the resources they need to rebuild their lives. This societal safety net includes healthcare, education, and employment services, all of which contribute to successful reintegration. The emphasis on social welfare reflects a societal belief in equity and the potential for redemption, supporting the idea that everyone deserves a second chance.

For other jurisdictions looking to adopt similar practices, several elements of the Scandinavian model offer valuable lessons. One is the implementation of educational programs within prisons. Education is a cornerstone of rehabilitation, providing inmates with the skills needed to succeed upon release. By offering educational opportunities, prisons can help inmates transition smoothly back into society, reducing the chances of reoffending. Community-based correctional facilities also present a viable alternative to traditional incarceration. These facilities emphasize community integration, allowing offenders to maintain their family connections and employment while serving their sentences. This model not only reduces the stigma associated with imprisonment but also prepares individuals for a successful reentry into society.

Norway's experience suggests that investing in rehabilitation can yield substantial rewards for both individuals and the society at large. The focus on humane treatment, education, and reintegration creates a cycle where former offenders become productive members of society rather than returning to criminal activity. While implementing the Norwegian model elsewhere may seem challenging, especially in countries with different cultural and legal backgrounds, it offers a powerful example of what is possible when a society prioritizes rehabilitation over retribution. The potential for positive change is significant, demonstrating that with the right support, most people can overcome their past and contribute positively to their communities.

The Use of Technology in Sentencing: A Global Perspective

In today's rapidly evolving world, technology has become entwined with the judicial process, reshaping how sentences are determined and implemented. One of the most significant advancements has been the integration of automated risk assessment tools, which use data algorithms to evaluate the likelihood of a defendant reoffending, providing judges with additional information to consider when deciding a sentence. While these tools were aimed to enhance judicial efficiency and fairness by offering objective assessments, they have also raised questions about the reliability and transparency of the algorithms used. Critics argue that these systems can perpetuate existing biases if the data fed into them are skewed or incomplete.

Virtual courtrooms and remote hearings have also emerged as technological solutions to streamline the judicial process. Particularly highlighted during the global pandemic, these innovations have allowed courts to function without physical presence, saving time and resources. They offer a level of accessibility that was previously unimaginable, enabling witnesses and defendants to participate from anywhere in the world. For students and policymakers, the implications are significant, as these tools could democratize access to the legal process. However, the transition to virtual platforms also presents challenges, such as ensuring data security and maintaining the integrity of legal proceedings.

The role of technology in sentencing is not without its complexities. On one hand, it promises increased transparency and consistency in judicial decisions by reducing human error and subjective biases. On the other hand, it raises concerns about privacy and data security, as sensitive personal data must be protected from breaches. Moreover, relying on technology can sometimes hinder the nuanced understanding that human judges bring to the courtroom. The balance between leveraging technology for efficiency and preserving the human element of justice is delicate and requires continuous evaluation.

Estonia is as a pioneering example of AI-driven sentencing algorithms, where technology assists in formulating sentences by analyzing a vast array of case data. These systems aim to standardize sentencing outcomes, reducing the disparities that might arise from human subjectivity. In New Zealand, electronic monitoring programs have been implemented as a means of tracking offenders outside of prison, allowing them to serve their sentences within the community while being closely monitored. This approach not only reduces incarceration costs but also allows offenders maintain family and employment ties, which are crucial for successful rehabilitation.

Despite the advantages of integrating technology into sentencing, ethical concerns must be addressed. One significant concern is the potential bias in algorithmic decision-making. If the data used to train these algorithms reflect societal biases, the outcomes may perpetuate those biases on a broader scale. For instance, studies have shown that some risk assessment tools predict higher recidivism rates for minority groups, raising questions about fairness and equality. Ensuring accountability and establishing robust oversight mechanisms are crucial to prevent such biases from influencing judicial outcomes.

Interactive Exercise: Evaluating Technology in Sentencing

Consider a hypothetical scenario where a risk assessment tool suggests a harsher sentence for a defendant based on historical data trends. Reflect on how you would address potential biases in the algorithm. What steps might you take to ensure a fair and unbiased sentencing process? Think about the trade-offs between technological efficiency and ethical integrity and how you would balance them in a real-world context.

As technology continues to transform the legal landscape, opportunities and challenges arise, and understanding these dynamics is vital for college students and policymakers. As you explore these innovations, consider their implications for fairness, efficiency, and the fundamental principles of justice that underpin the legal system.

Cultural Influences on Sentencing Practices

In the realm of justice, cultural norms exert considerable influence over sentencing practices, serving as a lens through which societies interpret crime and punishment. Imagine a courtroom in a collective society where the emphasis is on community harmony and the offender's role within the larger social fabric. Here, justice will not be just about the individual but about restoring balance within the community. In contrast, individualistic cultures prioritize personal accountability, with sentences often reflecting a focus on personal responsibility and deterrence. These cultural attitudes shape how societies perceive justice, influencing not only the length and type of sentences handed down but also the processes by which they are determined.

Multicultural societies face unique challenges in accommodating diverse cultural expectations within a single legal framework. The integration of customary law in Oceania is an illustrative example of situations where traditional practices coexist with modern legal systems. These societies strive to respect their cultural heritage while also ensuring that justice is administered fairly for all. Indigenous sentencing courts in Australia provide another instance of this balance, as they incorporate indigenous traditions and values into the sentencing process, allowing for the development of culturally relevant solutions that resonate with the communities involved. By respecting cultural diversity, such systems acknowledge the unique identities of their citizens, fostering a sense of inclusion and legitimacy in the justice process.

Culturally-informed sentencing approaches offer valuable insights into how justice systems can incorporate cultural understanding to enhance fairness. In New Zealand, Maori restorative practices exemplify this approach. These practices emphasize healing and reconciliation over punishment, reflecting the Maori ethos of collective well-being. By involving the offender, victim, and community in a collaborative process, these practices aim to repair harm and restore relationships. This model underscores the importance of cultural context in shaping effective sentencing strategies, highlighting how traditional wisdom can complement contemporary justice efforts. Such approaches not only address the needs of those directly involved but also strengthen community bonds, reinforcing a collective commitment to justice and rehabilitation.

However, the potential for cultural biases in sentencing remains a significant concern. Misunderstandings and misinterpretations of cultural practices can lead to biased outcomes, where defendants from minority cultures face unequal treatment. Several case studies have revealed instances where cultural differences have been misinterpreted, resulting in sentences that fail to consider the cultural context of the offense. In some cases, cultural practices have been mistakenly considered aggravating factors, leading to harsher penalties. These misunderstandings highlight the importance of cultural competence within the justice system, emphasizing the need for judges and legal practitioners to be aware of and sensitive to cultural nuances.

Consider a courtroom scenario where a defendant's cultural background is integral to understanding the motivations behind their actions. Without cultural awareness, there is a risk of imposing sentences that do not reflect the true nature of the offense. This can exacerbate existing disparities and undermine trust in the justice system. By fostering cultural competence and encouraging the inclusion of cultural perspectives in legal proceedings, justice systems can work toward more equitable outcomes. This involves organizing training for legal professionals, increasing representation of cultural minorities within the judiciary, and developing guidelines that account for cultural factors in sentencing decisions.

As cultural diversity continues to shape global societies, understanding its impact on sentencing practices becomes increasingly important. For those involved in the justice system, whether as students, policymakers, or practitioners, recognizing the role of culture in shaping legal outcomes is crucial and invites a broader dialogue on how justice can be administered in a way that respects and values cultural differences, ultimately contributing to a more inclusive and equitable legal landscape.

Global Innovations in Sentencing Reforms

Recently, the global landscape of criminal sentencing has witnessed a remarkable shift as countries rethink traditional punitive approaches and embrace innovative reforms. One significant trend has been the abolition of the death penalty in several countries. This move reflects a growing consensus that capital punishment is incompatible with modern principles of human rights and justice. Countries such as Mongolia and Burkina Faso have legislated to end the death penalty, joining a growing list of nations that have recognized the moral and ethical implications of state-sanctioned execution. The abolition of the death penalty is more than a legal reform; it represents a profound shift in societal values toward more humane and rehabilitative approaches to justice.

Another significant innovation in sentencing reforms is the decriminalization of certain offenses, particularly those related to drug use. Portugal stands out as a pioneering example, having decriminalized the possession of all drugs in 2001. This bold move redirected resources from punitive measures to public health interventions, emphasizing treatment over incarceration. The results have been impressive, with Portugal experiencing a dramatic reduction in drug-related deaths and a decrease in the overall prison population. This approach not only alleviates the burden on the criminal justice system but also addresses the root causes of addiction, offering a more compassionate and effective response to a complex social issue.

International organizations have played a pivotal role in promoting sentencing reforms, offering guidelines and support to nations seeking to modernize their justice systems. The United Nations, for example, has advocated for the use of non-custodial measures, encouraging countries to implement alternatives to imprisonment that focus on rehabilitation and reintegration. By providing frameworks and resources, international bodies help to harmonize sentencing practices across borders, fostering a global dialogue on best practices. These efforts are crucial in addressing the disparities and inefficiencies that often plague traditional sentencing models, paving the way for more equitable and effective justice systems worldwide.

The impact of these reforms on justice outcomes is significant. Countries that have embraced innovative sentencing practices have seen tangible improvements in their justice system. For instance, reforms that emphasize rehabilitation and non-custodial measures have contributed to reduced prison populations, alleviating overcrowding and allowing for better allocation of resources. This shift not only improves the conditions within correctional facilities but also enhances the potential for successful reintegration of ex-offenders into society. By focusing on rehabilitation rather than punishment, these reforms help to break the cycle of reoffending, ultimately leading to safer and more cohesive communities.

Case studies from various jurisdictions highlight the success of these reforms. Portugal's decriminalization of drugs, as mentioned earlier, serves as a model for other countries grappling with similar challenges. By shifting the focus away from criminalization to health, Portugal has reduced the stigma associated with drug use and improved access to treatment for users, offering valuable lessons for policymakers worldwide. In Canada, restorative justice initiatives, which promote healing and reconciliation between offenders and victims, have gained traction and have been particularly effective in indigenous communities where traditional practices of conflict resolution are integrated with contemporary justice approaches. The success of Canada's restorative justice efforts underscores the importance of culturally relevant solutions that resonate with the lived experiences of those involved.

These global innovations in sentencing reforms demonstrate the potential for transformative change within the justice system. By rethinking traditional approaches and embracing new ideas, countries can create a more equitable and effective system that prioritizes rehabilitation, reduces recidivism, and fosters social harmony. As nations continue to learn from one another and adapt to emerging challenges, the future of sentencing holds promise for a justice system that truly serves the needs of society.

The Future of Sentencing: International Trends and Predictions

Global sentencing practices are undergoing significant transformation, reflecting broader shifts in societal values and priorities. A key emerging trend is the increasing focus on human rights-based approaches to sentencing. This perspective emphasizes the dignity and rights of offenders, advocating for sentences that uphold fundamental human rights principles. This shift is driven by a growing recognition that although justice systems must punish offenders, they must also respect the inherent humanity of all individuals. This approach often includes the abolition of inhumane practices and an emphasis on rehabilitation and reintegration, aligning sentencing practices with international human rights standards.

Another emerging priority in the global justice landscape is the emphasis on victim restitution. This concept involves compensating victims for the harm they have suffered, i.e., acknowledging their pain and losses in a tangible way. Restitution can take many forms, from monetary compensation to community service that directly benefits those affected by crime. This focus on victims reflects a broader understanding of justice, one that seeks to also heal and restore rather than solely punish. It recognizes that justice is not only about addressing the wrong done to society but also about making amends to those who have been directly harmed.

International advocacy and movements are playing a crucial role in shaping future sentencing policies. The growing influence of climate justice movements, for instance, is beginning to impact environmental sentencing. As awareness of environmental issues increases, there is a push for sentences that reflect the severity and long-term impact of environmental crimes. These movements advocate for holding corporations and individuals accountable for actions that harm the planet, emphasizing the need for justice systems to address environmental wrongs with the same seriousness they do other crimes. This shift highlights the evolving nature of justice, as societies increasingly recognize the interconnectedness of ecological and social well-being.

The potential for cross-jurisdictional learning and adaptation remains significant. Global networks for judicial collaboration facilitate the sharing of best practices and innovations in sentencing, allowing countries to learn from each other's successes and challenges and promoting the adoption of effective strategies across borders. For instance, countries with successful rehabilitation programs can offer insights to those looking to reduce their recidivism rates. This cross-pollination of ideas fosters a more unified approach to justice, where lessons learned in one jurisdiction can inform and improve practices elsewhere.

However, the path forward is not without its challenges. Balancing technological advancements with ethical considerations presents a significant obstacle. While technology can enhance efficiency and consistency in sentencing, it also raises concerns about privacy and potential biases. Ensuring that these tools are used ethically and transparently will be crucial as they become more integrated into the justice process. Additionally, addressing global disparities in sentencing equity remains a pressing issue. Despite considerable progress, significant differences in sentencing practices persist between countries and within regions. Bridging these gaps requires concerted efforts to promote fairness and equality across all justice systems, ensuring that everyone receives the same treatment under the law regardless of geography or background.

As global sentencing practices continue to evolve, these trends and challenges highlight the dynamic nature of justice in the modern world. By embracing human rights, focusing on victim restitution, and learning from one another, justice systems can imbibe more equitable and effective approaches. The future of sentencing promises to be one of adaptation and innovation, where the lessons of the past inform the possibilities of tomorrow. In the next chapter, we will explore how these evolving practices are reshaping the landscape of criminal justice.

Chapter 8:
Reform and Future Directions

Imagine a courtroom where justice no longer wears the heavy cloak of rigidity but instead dons a mantle of reform and possibility. This transformation is not just a vision but a movement that has been gaining momentum over the past few decades. The roots of sentencing reform can be traced back to pivotal moments in history, one of which is the Sentencing Reform Act of 1984, which was a game-changer, establishing the United States Sentencing Commission and introducing guidelines intended to reduce disparity in federal sentences. Yet, it was just the beginning. Over time, influential court cases further shaped sentencing policy, challenging the status quo and inspiring a reevaluation of what justice means in a modern society. These cases have highlighted the need for a system that is fair as well as adaptable to the constantly changing moral and social landscape.

The evolution of reform efforts reflects a significant shift from punitive to rehabilitative approaches. In the past, the justice system mainly focused on punishment as the primary deterrent to crime. However, as civil rights movements gained traction, the conversation began to change. These movements highlighted the deep-rooted inequalities within the system, advocating for a justice approach that recognizes the potential for rehabilitation and redemption. Reform efforts have increasingly emphasized the importance of addressing the root causes of crime, such as poverty and lack of education, rather than solely focusing on punishment. This shift has led to the development of programs that prioritize rehabilitation over incarceration, aiming to reintegrate individuals into society as productive members.

Today, the landscape of sentencing reform continues to evolve, with current trends focusing on reducing mass incarceration and addressing racial disparities. The United States has the highest incarceration rate in the world, prompting urgent calls for change. Reform advocates argue that the system disproportionately affects minority communities, resulting in racial disparities that undermine the principles of justice. Consequently, there is a growing emphasis on implementing policies that aim to reduce the prison population while ensuring public safety. This includes revisiting mandatory minimum sentences and expanding opportunities for alternative sentencing, such as community service and rehabilitation programs. By addressing these issues, reform efforts aim to create a more equitable justice system that serves all citizens fairly.

Advocacy groups play a crucial role in driving reform, influencing both policy changes and public opinion. Organizations like The Sentencing Project have been at the helm of these efforts, conducting research and raising awareness about the injustices within the system. Their campaigns focus on educating the public and policymakers about the need for reform and highlighting the human and economic costs of mass incarceration. Grassroots movements also contribute significantly to this cause by mobilizing communities to demand legislative changes. These movements harness the power of collective action, demonstrating that when people come together, they can drive meaningful change. By engaging citizens in the reform process, advocacy groups help ensure that the voices of those most affected by the system are heard and considered while making policy decisions.

Reflection Section: Exploring Sentencing Reform

Reflect on your community and identify any local efforts aimed at sentencing reform. Consider how these efforts align with the broader trends discussed in this chapter. What role do advocacy groups play in your area, and how can you contribute to these initiatives?

Reflecting on these questions can help you understand the impact of reform efforts and inspire you to engage in meaningful action.

Exploring Alternatives to Incarceration

Imagine standing at the crossroads of justice, where the traditional path of incarceration stretches out, worn and familiar, yet fraught with limitations. Incarceration, with its high costs and questionable effectiveness in reducing recidivism, often fails to deliver on its promise of rehabilitation. The financial burden alone is staggering, with billions spent annually to maintain prison systems that, paradoxically, can turn first-time offenders into hardened criminals by exposing them to a culture of crime. The traditional path of incarceration often leads to overcrowded prisons, where resources are stretched thin and rehabilitation becomes a distant ideal rather than a reality. The pressing need for alternatives is clear, and a shift toward solutions that address the root causes of crime rather than simply punishing the act is required.

Alternative sentencing offers a promising divergence from traditional incarceration. For instance, electronic monitoring programs, which use technology, such as GPS tracking, to enforce house arrest, allow offenders to maintain employment and family connections while serving their sentences. These programs provide a cost-effective way to ensure compliance without the need for costly prison space. Community service and restitution further extend this promise, enabling offenders to give back to society and make amends for their actions. These alternatives not only reduce the financial strain on the justice system but also foster a sense of responsibility and accountability in offenders.

Drug treatment and rehabilitation programs stand out as particularly effective alternatives, especially for non-violent offenders. By focusing on the issues underlying addiction, these programs aim to break the cycle of crime and recidivism. Participants receive counseling, education, and support to overcome their dependencies, significantly lowering their likelihood of reoffending. Studies have consistently shown that offenders who complete drug treatment programs have lower recidivism rates than those who serve traditional prison sentences. The emphasis on healing rather than punishment aligns with modern understandings of addiction as a health issue deserving of compassion and support rather than mere condemnation.

Restorative justice, which involves bringing offenders and victims together to find a resolution, has also been shown to reduce recidivism rates. This approach fosters dialogue and understanding, encouraging offenders to take responsibility for their actions and victims to find closure. Similarly, probation programs have demonstrated increased compliance by offenders, when coupled with support services such as job training and mental health counseling. These services address the socio-economic factors that often contribute to criminal behavior, creating a holistic approach to justice that benefits both the individual and society.

Despite their promise, implementing alternative sentencing is challenging. Resistance from traditional justice stakeholders, who may view these alternatives as too lenient, can slow progress. There is a deeply ingrained belief that harsh punishment equals justice, a mindset that is difficult to change. Additionally, funding and resource limitations pose significant obstacles. Many programs require substantial upfront investment to establish infrastructure and train personnel, which can deter policymakers from adopting these approaches. The challenge lies in demonstrating the long-term cost savings and societal benefits of these alternatives and convincing stakeholders of their value.

The path toward embracing alternative sentencing is fraught with hurdles, yet its potential to transform the justice system is immense. As you consider these alternatives, reflect on the broader implications of justice beyond punishment. Think about how these approaches could reshape the future of sentencing, offering a more humane and effective way of achieving justice. The possibilities are vast, inviting a reimagining of what justice could be.

The Role of Community-Based Programs in Sentencing

Picture a bustling neighborhood, vibrant and full of life, where justice is not just a distant courtroom encounter but a community endeavor. Community-based sentencing programs embody this vision by integrating the principles of rehabilitation and reintegration right where individuals live, focusing on reshaping lives through local support. These programs aim to repair the fabric of communities by directly involving members in the justice process. Unlike conventional incarceration, which often alienates offenders, community-based approaches seek to reconnect them with the very fabric of society through accountability and support. This method acknowledges that sustainable change often begins at home, where individuals find the encouragement needed to turn their lives around.

One shining example of such an initiative is the Harlem Community Justice Center. This program offers a holistic approach to justice, addressing not just the legal issues but also the underlying social and economic challenges faced by participants. By providing services like housing assistance, job training, and mental health support, the center helps reduce recidivism and fosters long-term positive outcomes. Similarly, the Circles of Support and Accountability (CoSA) model pairs former offenders with community volunteers who offer guidance and friendship. This relationship helps offenders reintegrate into society and reduces their likelihood of reoffending. These programs exemplify how community engagement can transform lives, promote safety, and reduce crime.

The benefits of involving communities in the sentencing process extend beyond the individuals directly involved. Community-based programs strengthen community ties, creating a supportive network that encourages positive behavior. This network provides a safety net for individuals as they navigate the complexities of reintegration, offering resources tailored to their unique needs. By engaging local stakeholders, these programs foster a sense of shared responsibility for public safety, shifting the focus from punishment to prevention. The collaborative nature of these efforts makes them uniquely effective, as they draw on the strengths and resources of the community to address the root causes of crime.

Despite their promise, sustaining and expanding the impact of community-based programs is significantly challenging, as securing long-term funding is a particular obstacle. Many initiatives rely on grants and donations, making them vulnerable to economic fluctuations and changes in political priorities. Without stable financial support, these programs struggle to maintain the level of service and outreach necessary for success. Additionally, gaining community buy-in and support can be difficult. Some community members may be skeptical of the programs' effectiveness or fear that they could compromise safety. Therefore, overcoming these concerns requires ongoing education and engagement to demonstrate the tangible benefits of community-based justice.

Reflection Section: Community Engagement in Justice

Consider your own community and the potential for implementing or supporting community-based sentencing programs. Reflect on the resources and networks available that could be leveraged to support such initiatives. What challenges might you face in gaining community buy-in, and how would you address them? Reflecting on these can inspire you to find ways to engage your community in the justice process, fostering a collaborative approach to safety and rehabilitation.

Crafting Policies for Equitable Sentencing

In the realm of justice, equitable sentencing stands as a beacon of fairness, aiming to tailor punishment to both the crime and the unique circumstances of the offender. True equity in sentencing means that justice is not a one-size-fits-all solution but a nuanced approach that considers individual backgrounds, motivations, and the broader social context. This involves a commitment to recognizing the diverse factors that contribute to each case, such as mental health, socio-economic status, and even cultural background. The goal is to eliminate biases that may arise due to race or economic disparity, ensuring that each sentence is just and fitting. Crafting policies with this vision requires a deliberate examination of how systemic biases have historically influenced sentencing and a resolute effort to address these issues head-on.

One strategy for achieving equitable sentencing is using impact assessments in policy development. These assessments analyze how proposed sentencing policies might affect different demographic groups, highlighting potential disparities before they become entrenched. By evaluating the effects of policies in advance, lawmakers can adjust their approaches to minimize unintended consequences. Another key element is involving diverse stakeholders in policy-making, including legal experts as well as representatives from communities most affected by sentencing practices. Their insights ensure that policies are realistic and relevant to the populations they impact. Such collaboration fosters a more inclusive dialogue, where varied perspectives contribute to a fuller understanding of justice and equity.

Successful models of equitable sentencing policy can be found in various jurisdictions, with New Zealand being a notable example.

This country's approach to culturally-responsive sentencing considers the cultural context of offenders, particularly within its indigenous Maori population, and integrates traditional Maori restorative practices, emphasizing healing and community involvement over punitive measures. By acknowledging cultural heritage and values, New Zealand has developed a system that respects diversity while promoting rehabilitation. Such practices highlight the importance of tailoring sentencing to fit the cultural and social realities of a population, providing a template for other jurisdictions seeking to enhance equity in justice.

Data and research play vital roles in shaping equitable sentencing policies. Utilizing sentencing data analytics allows policymakers to identify trends, evaluate the effectiveness of current practices, and pinpoint areas needing reform. These analytics provide a quantitative foundation for policy decisions, ensuring that changes are evidence-based rather than reactive. Ongoing evaluation and adjustment of policies are equally crucial because as societal norms and legal landscapes evolve, so too must the policies that govern them. Regularly reviewing sentencing outcomes helps maintain alignment with contemporary values and needs, fostering a justice system that is both responsive and responsible.

In crafting equitable sentencing policies, the focus is on creating a framework that supports justice and fairness across all societal strata. This involves a conscious effort to dismantle systemic biases and promote individualized consideration. By integrating diverse voices and leveraging data-driven insights, we can move toward a future where sentencing reflects both the letter and spirit of justice. The journey to achieving true equity is ongoing and requires vigilance, adaptability, and a commitment to continuous improvement.

The Impact of Legislative Changes on Sentencing Practices

Consider the transformation within the United States criminal justice system, marked by legislative shifts aimed at reshaping sentencing practices. The First Step Act, passed in 2018, stands out as a landmark reform in this context. This bipartisan legislation was crafted with the intent to reduce the federal prison population and address systemic inequities. Making the Fair Sentencing Act of 2010 retroactive allowed for the reevaluation of sentences for those convicted of crack cocaine offenses, a move that addressed longstanding racial disparities. Moreover, the Act expanded earned time credits for inmates, offering incentives for their participation in rehabilitative programs aimed at reducing recidivism. In its wake, over 30,000 individuals were released early, signaling a shift toward a more rehabilitative and equitable approach.

While the First Step Act was designed to overhaul certain punitive elements, it has brought both intended and unintended consequences. On one hand, the reduction in mandatory minimum sentences has given judges increased discretion, enabling them to consider individual circumstances more fully. This change has led to more nuanced sentencing, reflecting a move away from the rigid frameworks that previously dominated. On the other hand, changes in parole eligibility have sparked debates about public safety and the balance between rehabilitation and accountability. Critics argue that without adequate support systems, early release might not always lead to successful reintegration. The law's implementation has also highlighted challenges, such as slow processing and insufficient access to rehabilitative programming, which can hinder its effectiveness.

The political dynamics surrounding legislative reform play a critical role in shaping sentencing laws. While the First Step Act is a product of bipartisan efforts, reflecting a rare consensus across party lines, political agendas often influence the pace and direction of reform. Lawmakers' differing priorities can lead to compromises that dilute the impact of legislative changes. For instance, while reforms may aim to reduce excessive sentencing, they must also address concerns about crime rates and public safety, which are often central to political discourse. Navigating these dynamics requires a delicate balancing act, where the push for progress aligns with the realities of political negotiation.

Assessing the effectiveness of recent legislative reforms requires examining both statistical outcomes and the lived experiences of those affected. The First Step Act's impact can be seen in the reduced recidivism rates noticed among those released under its provisions, contrasting sharply with the broader federal rate. However, challenges remain, such as ensuring consistent access to programs that support successful reentry. Community case studies reveal mixed outcomes, with some areas experiencing positive changes in reintegration support and others struggling with resource limitations. These disparities underscore the need for continued attention to implementation, ensuring that legislative intentions translate into meaningful change on the ground.

Innovative Approaches to Sentencing: The Path Forward

Imagine a courtroom enhanced by technology, a space where traditional methods meet cutting-edge innovations. This is becoming a reality as global jurisdictions explore new approaches to sentencing that promise to reshape the justice system. One such innovation is the use of virtual reality (VR) in offender rehabilitation. VR allows offenders to engage in immersive scenarios that simulate real-world challenges, providing them with opportunities to practice decision-making and emotional regulation in a controlled environment. By offering a safe space to confront and modify behaviors, VR can play a crucial role in reducing recidivism and supporting rehabilitation efforts.

Another frontier in sentencing innovation is the adoption of artificial intelligence (AI) for risk assessment and decision-making. AI systems analyze vast datasets to evaluate an offender's likelihood of reoffending, providing judges with data-based insights to inform their sentencing decisions. These tools aim to enhance the efficiency and fairness of the justice process by removing human biases and focusing on objective criteria. However, AI implementation in sentencing is not without controversy, as concerns about ethical implications and privacy have arisen since these systems require access to sensitive personal data and can perpetuate existing biases if not carefully managed. Balancing technological advancement with ethical considerations is critical to ensuring that AI serves the cause of justice effectively.

Globally, pilot programs are testing these new sentencing models, offering glimpses into the future of justice. For instance, several jurisdictions are experimenting with algorithm-driven sentencing, where AI algorithms assist judges in determining appropriate penalties based on analyzed case data. These pilot programs aim to evaluate the potential of AI to streamline sentencing while maintaining accuracy and fairness. Early results show promise, with some regions reporting more consistent sentencing outcomes and reduced case processing times. However, these programs also highlight the need for continuous oversight and human involvement to address the nuances of each case that algorithms may overlook.

Looking ahead, the integration of technology with human oversight presents a promising path for further sentencing reform. By combining the analytical power of AI with the empathy and judgment of human decision-makers, the justice system can achieve a more balanced approach to sentencing. This hybrid model can help mitigate the risks associated with fully automated decision-making, ensuring that technology complements rather than replaces human discretion. Additionally, a focus on individualized and restorative justice is crucial for future innovations. Tailoring sentences to the specific circumstances of each offender and emphasizing rehabilitation over punishment can foster more equitable outcomes and support long-term societal well-being.

As these innovations unfold, they pave the way for a justice system that is more responsive to the complexities of modern society. By embracing new technologies and approaches, we can enhance the fairness and effectiveness of sentencing, moving closer to a system that truly reflects the values of justice and equity. The path forward is one of exploration and adaptation, calling for collaboration among policymakers, technologists, and communities to shape a future where justice is accessible, fair, and forward-thinking.

Conclusion

As we reach the end of our journey together through the complex landscape of criminal sentencing, we hope this book has helped unravel the intricacies of a process that has long been shrouded in mystery. Our aim was to provide a resource that college students and policymakers could find both informative and engaging, sparking informed discussions and inspiring thoughtful change.

In our exploration, we have delved into the foundational principles of sentencing, such as deterrence, retribution, rehabilitation, and restoration. We have also examined the sentencing process in detail, considering the legal guidelines, discretion wielded by judges, and societal factors that influence decisions. Through real-world case studies, we have seen how these principles play out in diverse contexts, offering a window into the practical application of theoretical concepts.

More importantly, we have addressed the impact of racial and systemic biases on sentencing, recognizing the disparities that persist within the justice system. From examining high-profile cases to understanding the subtleties of judicial discretion, these discussions highlight the urgent need for reform and serve as a reminder that while the law strives for objectivity, human prejudice can imperceptibly shape outcomes.

The insights gained from exploring ethical and social considerations have been profound. The role of media, for example, in shaping public perceptions cannot be understated, as media narratives often color our understanding of justice, demanding a critical examination of how crime and punishment are portrayed. Moreover, viewing sentencing through a global lens reveals diverse practices and philosophies, challenging us to learn from other systems and consider innovative approaches.

Reflecting on the case studies presented, we have observed how sentencing can vary dramatically based on the circumstances of each case. The stories told of individuals caught in the web of the justice system illustrate both the potential for justice and the pitfalls of a one-size-fits-all approach. These narratives underscore the importance of tailoring sentences to fit the crime and individual, recognizing the myriad factors at play.

There is no denying the importance of reform in achieving a fairer, more equitable justice system. Innovative approaches, such as restorative justice and alternative sentencing, offer promising paths forward, as they address the current challenges in the justice system and highlight future directions that prioritize rehabilitation over mere punishment.

Understanding sentencing as a complex interplay of social, ethical, and cultural factors that demands nuanced analysis and thoughtful reform, rather than just a legal process, is vital. As a reader, your role extends beyond absorbing information. we urge you to engage actively in discussions about sentencing reform, using the knowledge gained here to advocate for change, challenge existing norms, and contribute to a more just and equitable system.

On a personal note, the journey of writing this book has been both enlightening and rewarding, and we hope it leaves a lasting impact on you, inspiring you to engage more deeply with the justice system and fueling a broader discourse on reform. The complexities of sentencing are vast, but with continued learning and advocacy, we can work toward meaningful change.

In conclusion, we invite you to keep exploring. Seek out additional resources, engage with advocacy groups, and continue to question and reflect on the themes we have discussed. The work of reform is ongoing, and every voice matters in the pursuit of justice.

Finally, we would like to leave you with this thought: Justice is not a destination but a journey—a process of continuous improvement and reflection. How will you contribute to shaping the future of sentencing? Will you be a catalyst for change? The path is yours to forge, and the possibilities are endless.

About the Authors

Professors Lisa Stolzenberg and Stewart D'Alessio's journey in the dynamic field of criminology resembles the chapters of a compelling crime novel. Individually, they are formidable scholars; together, they have redefined the boundaries of criminological research. Their collaborative journey highlights the confluence of their passions and demonstrates the power of synergy in academic pursuits.

Upon completing their undergraduate studies, Stolzenberg and D'Alessio met in 1986 at Florida State University while pursuing postgraduate degrees in criminology. A casual conversation over pizza evolved into a brainstorming session and a collaborative partnership that has lasted nearly four decades. After initially accepting faculty positions at Indiana-Purdue University Fort Wayne, they relocated to Florida International University (FIU) in Miami, where they spent their childhood years. Today, they are tenured criminology professors at FIU's Steven J. Green School of International and Public Affairs.

Drs. Stolzenberg and D'Alessio's combined expertise and passion for criminology have led to significant contributions in the fields of criminology and criminal justice. Working in tandem, they have published numerous books and influential scholarly articles on race and crime, criminal sentencing, and criminal justice policy. They were also instrumental in developing two unique degree programs in the United States: the Ph.D. in International Crime and Justice and the Bachelor of Science in Crime Science.

Today, criminologists worldwide are inspired by their dedication, innovative spirit, and ability to break down silos in the pursuit of knowledge. Their story is a testament to the power of collaboration and the profound impact committed individuals can have when they unite to pursue knowledge and justice.

References

Alexander, M. (2010, December 6). *The new Jim Crow*. The American Prospect. https://prospect.org/special-report/new-jim-crow/

Berman, J. S. (2021, March 18). *What happens at sentencing?* NOLO. https://www.nolo.com/legal-encyclopedia/what-happens-sentencing.html

Brodowicz, M. (Ed.). (2024, July 25). *The impact of media coverage on public perception in high-profile murder cases*. https://aithor.com/essay-examples/the-impact-of-media-coverage-on-public-perception-in-high-profile-murder-cases

Clinton, O. L. (1993). Cultural differences and sentencing departures. *Federal Sentencing Reporter*, *5*(6), 348-352. https://www.jstor.org/stable/20639611

Chen, X. (2022). Deep learning-based intelligent robot in sentencing – PMC. *Frontiers in Psychology*, *13*, 901796. https://www.ncbi.nlm.nih.gov/pmc/articles/PMC9341297/

Community violence intervention success stories. https://www.americanprogress.org/article/community-violence-intervention-success-stories/

Drury, M., & Janice, B. (2023, November 21). *Retributive criminal justice | Definition, law & examples*. Study.com. https://study.com/learn/lesson/retributive-justice-theory-law-examples.html?srsltid=AfmBOorwG_vAJrOIj0l05XnFECmSNuBg8fhIF9l_yiGyu-0PL2PW2pyC

Electronic Privacy Information Center. *AI in the criminal justice system.* https://epic.org/issues/ai/ai-in-the-criminal-justice-system/

Executive summary. U.S. Sentencing Commission. https://www.ussc.gov/sites/default/files/pdf/research-and-publications/research-projects-and-surveys/miscellaneous/15-year-study/executive_summary_and_preface.pdf

Federal Judicial Center. *Sentencing.* Judiciaries Worldwide. http://judiciariesworldwide.fjc.gov/sentencing

First Step Alliance. (2022, January 3). *What we can learn from Norway's prison system: Rehabilitation & recidivism.* https://www.firststepalliance.org/post/norway-prison-system-lessons

Fitzmaurice, C., & Pease, K. (1985). *Psychology of judicial sentencing* (Report No. 103242). https://www.ojp.gov/ncjrs/virtual-library/abstracts/psychology-judicial-sentencing

Government of Canada. (2022, August 26). *The effectiveness of restorative justice practices: A meta-analysis.* https://www.justice.gc.ca/eng/rp-pr/csj-sjc/jsp-sjp/rp01_1-dr01_1/p5.html

Hewitt, J. (2016). Fifty shades of gray: Sentencing trends in major white-collar cases. *The Yale Law Journal, 125*(4), 796-1149. https://www.yalelawjournal.org/note/fifty-shades-of-gray-sentencing-trends-in-major-white-collar-cases

Kaina, R. (2018, October). *Media's influence on the perception of criminal justice.* Crime and Justice Research Alliance. https://crimeandjusticeresearchalliance.org/rsrch/medias-influence-on-the-perception-of-criminal-justice/

LaBrie, R. (2022, May 21). *White-collar crime: Diversity and discrimination in sentencing.* Honors Project. https://digitalcommons.spu.edu/ cgi/viewcontent.cgi?article=1173&context=honorsprojects

Martin, E. (2017, March 1). *Hidden consequences: The impact of incarceration on dependent children.* National Institute of Justice. https://nij.ojp.gov/topics/articles/hidden-consequences-impact-incarceration-dependent-children

Mitchell, O., & MacKenzie, D. L. (2004, December). *The relationship between race, ethnicity, and sentencing outcomes: A meta-analysis of sentencing research* (Report No. 208129). https://www.ojp.gov/ pdffiles1/nij/grants/208129.pdf

National Centre for State Courts. *Helping courts address implicit bias: Strategies to reduce the influence of implicit bias.* https://www.ccf.ny.gov/files/2215/2044/3779/Helping_courts_reduc e_the_influence_of_implicit_bias.pdf

Nellis, A. (2024, February 14). *How mandatory minimums perpetuate mass incarceration and what to do about it.* The Sentencing Project. https://www.sentencingproject.org/fact-sheet/how-mandatory-minimums-perpetuate-mass-incarceration-and-what-to-do-about-it/

Nellis, A., & Komar, L. (2023, August 22). *The First Step Act: Ending mass incarceration in federal prisons.* The Sentencing Project. https://www.sentencingproject.org/policy-brief/the-first-step-act-ending-mass-incarceration-in-federal-prisons/

Newman, A. (). *The role of victim impact statements in sentencing* https://www.derstinebariteau.com/blog/the-role-of-victim-impact-statements-in-sentencing

Racial bias in crime reporting | On the media. https://www.wnycstudios.org/podcasts/otm/segments/crime-reporting-racial-bias

Ratner, M. A. (2016). *Judicial ethical integrity: Challenges and solutions.* UC Hastings Scholarship Repository. https://repository.uclawsf.edu/cgi/viewcontent.cgi?article=2421&context=faculty_scholarship

Roberts, J. V., & Doo, A. N. (1990). News media influences on public views of sentencing. *Law and Human Behavior*, *14*(5), 451-458. https://ojp.gov/ncjrs/virtual-library/abstracts/news-media-influences-public-views-sentencing

Seigle, E., Walsh, N., & Weber, J. (2014). *Reducing juvenile recidivism.* The Council of State Governments Justice Center. https://csgjusticecenter.org/publications/reducing-juvenile-recidivism/

Sentencing reform. https://www.aclu.org/issues/smart-justice/sentencing-reform

Tomlinson, K. D. (2016). An examination of deterrence theory: Where do we stand? *Federal Probation Journal, 80*(3), 33-38. https://www.uscourts.gov/sites/default/files/80_3_4_0.pdf

United States Sentencing Commission. (2022). An *overview of the federal sentencing guidelines.* https://www.ussc.gov/sites/default/files/pdf/about/overview/Overview_Federal_Sentencing_Guidelines.pdf

United States Sentencing Commission. (2023, November 14). *2023 Demographic differences in federal sentencing.* https://www.ussc.gov/

research/research-reports/2023-demographic-differences-federal-sentencing

Walsh, A. (1985). Role of the probation officer in the sentencing process independent professional of judicial hack? *Criminal Justice and Behavior*, *12*(3), 289-303. https://ojp.gov/ncjrs/virtual-library/abstracts/role-probation-officer-sentencing-process-independent-professional

www.ingramcontent.com/pod-product-compliance
Lightning Source LLC
Chambersburg PA
CBHW070254290326
41930CB00041B/2519

* 9 7 8 1 9 3 6 6 5 1 1 7 7 *